How the Information Revolution Remade Business and the Economy

How the Information Revolution Remade Business and the Economy

A Roadmap for Progress of the Semiconductor Industry

Apek Mulay

BEP BUSINESS EXPERT PRESS

How the Information Revolution Remade Business and the Economy:
A Roadmap for Progress of the Semiconductor Industry
Copyright © Business Expert Press, LLC, 2017.

First published in 2017 by
Business Expert Press, LLC
222 East 46th Street, New York, NY 10017
www.businessexpertpress.com

ISBN-13: 978-1-63157-589-1 (print)
ISBN-13: 978-1-63157-590-7 (e-book)

Business Expert Press Economics Collection

Collection ISSN: 2163-761X (print)
Collection ISSN: 2163-7628 (electronic)

Cover and interior design by S4Carlisle Publishing Services
Private Ltd., Chennai, India

First edition: 2017

10 9 8 7 6 5 4 3 2 1

Printed in the United States of America

Abstract

To comprehend the impact of technology on the ways in which business practices are changing is an intimidating subject of study for any student of engineering, business, or economics. Businesses essentially exist in order to provide goods and services to their customers. In that milieu, the growth of any business depends heavily on the ever-increasing number of consumers for its products or services. In other words, consumer purchasing power is directly related to the Return on Investments (RoI) of any business.

The exponential technological progress over the last 50 years has been associated with the rapid progress of Moore's law in the global semiconductor industry. This has resulted in an exponential growth in productivity as well as increased automation in order to reduce the costs of operation for businesses. On the one hand, the ever-growing productivity of machines has reduced the requirements for manual labor. But, on the other hand, the huge unemployment that has been created through reduction of workforce as a result of automation has reduced the consumer purchasing power in the economy, which is indirectly hurting the RoI from the increased growth in productivity of machines. All these bring any further progress of Moore's law to a standstill.

Hence, the industry body—*International Technology Roadmap for Semiconductors* (ITRS)—has proposed *"More-than-Moore"* and *"Beyond CMOS"* as new drivers to further drive the technological progress of Moore's law, in order to continue the growth of global semiconductor industry as well as to usher the fourth industrial revolution in the form of "the Internet of Things" (IoT). This book essentially argues that the progress of Moore's law is coming to a standstill due to ignorance of common sense macroeconomics while driving the growth of the global semiconductor industry for the last half a century. It also provides a blueprint for sustaining the progress of the semiconductor industry as well as the broader economy and benefits from the growth in productivity of machines with new drivers of *"More than Moore"* and *"Beyond CMOS."*

It envisions this goal by proposing reforms in existing business practices to have a free market balanced macroeconomic growth. To summarize my proposed reforms, for Moore's law to progress both supply and demand have to grow. The supply in economy comes from productivity of workforce and demand comes from their wages. Hence, free markets should ensure that wages should automatically catch up with ever-growing technological productivity with a minimal government intervention. To avoid automation from destroying jobs in an economy, the working hours of workforce could be reduced during waning phase of economy and increased during its waxing phase so that the workers can achieve the desired production target in fewer working hours. Their freed-up time from it could be used for leisure, R&D, vocational training, etc.

This book is appropriate for students taking an introductory course about economics of semiconductor industry, MBAs, and business professionals interested in applying the fundamentals of a free market economy toward the growth of knowledge-based economy. It is also a useful book for macroeconomic policy makers, who are eagerly looking for a free market approach to revive their stagnating economies as well as to usher the fourth industrial revolution of IoT in their respective economies.

Keywords

Beyond CMOS, Capitalism and free markets, Chinese economy and semiconductor industry, Industry 4.0, Internet of Things (IoT), mass capitalism, maximum amenities, minimum necessities, Moore's law, 450-mm silicon wafers, More-than-Moore, power through collaboration, virtual IDM.

Contents

Foreword

It is a pleasure to read author Apek Mulay's contributions to the expanding research and development on economic approaches that incorporate the power of collaboration. The author's vision arises out of his work with the semiconductor and technology industry. He presents the case that declarations of the demise of Moore's law are premature. He proposes an economic approach designed to maintain the potency of Moore's law and sustain continued high RoI in the semiconductor and technology sector.

His mass capitalism vision proposes a shift from "individualized capitalism" to "collaborative capitalism." It takes into account the often-ignored yet essential macroeconomic parameters impacting Moore's law and semiconductors. Diminished consumer purchasing power and "crony capitalism" jeopardize the efficiency of Moore's law. Maintaining consumer purchasing power is essential to sustaining RoIs in the semiconductor and technology sectors. He calls for eliminating the supply–demand gap by eliminating the wage–productivity gap.

The author incorporates macroeconomic parameters in the formulation of growth drivers and business models for the semiconductor industry, and proposes an ecosystem for the IoT "fourth industrial revolution." The semiconductor industry is a keystone contributor to the ecosystem and to overall economic prosperity. As is to be expected in collaboration-based economic system, the benefits for one economic sector radiate far and wide to benefit other sectors. Thus, the author's vision reinvigorates not only technological investment and development for semiconductor companies, but also for the broader economy. His approach is designed to help usher in a golden age of technological progress and overcome the global economy's stagnation that lingers from the 2008 Great Recession.

The author proposes replacing demand-restraining and exploitative reliance upon debt and supply-side economics. He offers the concepts of "minimum necessities" and "maximum amenities" as more effective key drivers of economic demand, sustainable economic growth, and rising living standards, as well as for empowering entire populations.

One of the pivotal factors that can drive the success of approaches such as Mr. Mulay's is the utilization of the power of collaboration. The author builds upon the work of his two previous books that involve deep collaboration between semiconductor companies. His vision involves a collaborative ecosystem operating for the overall economy as well as the semiconductor industry; a shift away from "crony capitalism" to free market *mass capitalism*; greater use of collaborative business models and collaborative corporate structures; collaborative R&D ventures; collaborative utilization of infrastructure and resources; collaboration between companies, academia, and government; as well as collaboration between consumers and producers.

The author envisions that his collaborative ecosystem can boost consumer purchasing power and economic demand, lower income taxes, spur growth across wider swaths of the economic system, make growth more sustainable, cure mass poverty, address the critical needs of a growing world population, and enable a much larger number of people to participate in the resulting prosperity. Achieving these ambitious goals will require an economic system along the lines that Mr. Mulay proposes—one that is based upon and fully utilizes power through collaboration.

Stephen Willis, PhD
Author of Power through Collaboration
www.powerthroughcollaboration.com

Preface

Thomas Kuhn in his fascinating book *The Structure of Scientific Revolutions* (1962) had coined the term "paradigm shift." In that volume, he described that the scientific communities function within a paradigm, largely making incremental advances within that shared understood paradigm until there is a sudden and unpredictable shift to a new model or paradigm. The progress of Moore's law has had an unprecedented impact not just on the progress of the U.S. semiconductor industry but on the broader U.S. economy. An observation of Gordon E. Moore has played an important role in driving the roadmap for the growth of the semiconductor industry for the last half a century and has turned out to be one of the most transformative events in human history.

This doubling of the number of transistors on an integrated circuit has resulted in approximately 40 percent faster speed and 50 percent more efficiency of electronic products every generation of the progress of Moore's law. This has increased the technological productivity as well as profitability for not only the semiconductor industry but for the overall economy. The closely connected world through the Internet would not have been possible without the progress of Moore's law. Moore's law has played an important role in the growth of GDP by an exponential growth of electronic equipment market and related sectors in a broader global economy. Most of the companies listed on the S&P 500 such as Facebook, Amazon, Google, Adobe, Apple, etc. would not have existed had there not been such a rapid progress of Moore's law.

Now, the high costs of scaling have started to threaten the continued progress from any further evolution of Moore's law and its ability to sustain the progress of today's knowledge-based economy. As industry experts believe that it would be the economics of shrinking transistor dimensions that would play an important role in sustaining this progress of Moore's law, the ITRS has come up with new drivers for *More-than-Moore* and *Beyond CMOS* to continue the progress of the global semiconductor industry. The progress of global semiconductor industry in driving the progress of Moore's law has been driven by a progress of supply-side economics since the 1980s. The global semiconductor industry has thus made incremental advances within a shared understood paradigm of supply-side economics. In order to ensure a profitability of any new project like *More-than-Moore* and *Beyond CMOS*, a good macroeconomic policy is essential because the Return on Investment (RoI) on any project depends on the health of the macroeconomy or the basic forces of supply and demand.

More-than-Moore is a facet of the semiconductor microelectronics that complements the digital part of the integrated systems. More specifically, the *More-than-Moore* approach allows for the non-digital functionalities to be integrated into microelectronic products to improve productivity. This approach may not scale according to Moore's law, but provides an additional value to the products. It helps in the migration from the system board level into the package called as System in Package (SiP) or onto the chip called as System on Chip (SoC).

The ongoing global macroeconomic crisis that is the result of a faulty monetary policy of the central banks presents a sudden and an unpredictable shift for the semiconductor industry to sustain its progress. A good macroeconomic policy calls for a new business model to boost consumer demand in the economy for sustaining the progress of *More-than-Moore* and *Beyond CMOS*. It calls for a thoughtful departure from the existing macroeconomic policies that have resulted in an ongoing global macroeconomic crisis, in order to lead the global semiconductor industry and the global economy to its next level of innovation and financial success. That is exactly where this book comes in. It analyzes the roadmap proposed by ITRS for *More-than-Moore* and *Beyond CMOS* and presents a sustainable blueprint to measure the progress on this planned roadmap for the future. Without a goal to boost economic demand in order to sustain a consumption of manufactured electronics, any further growth of the global semiconductor industry would not only be sustainable but would also not be very profitable.

Chapter 1 exposes the reader to the magic of 50 years of progress of Moore's law based on the progress of knowledge-based economy in the United States and around the world. It demonstrates the importance of being able to sustain this progress in order to continue benefiting humans from new technological innovations and productivity. It provides evolution of different business models in the semiconductor industry with the progress of Moore's law. Chapter 2 highlights the importance of ensuring a good RoI for driving more investments into the economy for sustaining the progress of Moore's law. Chapter 3 helps the reader understand the strategic significance of having government support for establishing a state-of-the-art semiconductor manufacturing industry in any economy. It analyzes the rise of the Chinese semiconductor industry driven by an unsustainable progress of Moore's law in the US semiconductor industry and also presents the causes of an economic crash of Chinese stock markets in summer of 2015 in spite of a rapid progress of its semiconductor industry due to wage–productivity gap resulting from an excessive government intervention into the economy.

Chapter 4 provides an in-depth analysis of the future road map of semiconductor industry proposed by ITRS based on the committee's recommendations. It also furnishes the reader with the history about ITRS. Chapter 5 evaluates the two major business models prevalent in the global semiconductor industry, viz. fabless-foundry and integrated device manufacturer (IDM) and highlights the advantages as well as the disadvantages from a macroeconomic perspective. Chapter 6 elaborates on the various drivers proposed by the ITRS for driving the progress of *More-than-Moore* and *Beyond CMOS*. Chapter 7 offers practical solutions for sustaining the progress of *More-than-Moore* and *Beyond CMOS* with free market economic theory of *mass capitalism*. Chapter 8 then quantifies the measurement of this progress so as to have a well-defined single goal for driving any further progress of the semiconductor industry.

Chapter 9 educates the reader about the demand-side economic drivers of "minimum necessities" and "maximum amenities" for driving a sustainable progress of Moore's law based on *More-than-Moore* and *Beyond CMOS*. Chapter 10 then addresses practical solutions to offer a broader economic prosperity by increased economic demand for consumer electronics with a continued progress of *More-than-Moore* and *Beyond CMOS*. Chapter 11 then addresses the holistic design of the entire semiconductor ecosystem for ushering in the fourth industrial revolution in the form of the *Internet of Things* (*IoT*). It also verifies whether the designed *IoT* ecosystem complies with the five fundamental factors of the free market economic theory of *mass capitalism* when it includes drivers for *More-than-Moore* and *Beyond CMOS*. Last but not the least, in the Appendix, I offer a virtual macroeconomic makeover of some opinionated technology guru pontifications about the *IoT*.

Acknowledgments

I owe my greatest intellectual debt to a great neohumanist Shrii Prabhat Ranjan Sarkar who continues to inspire me to accelerate the speed of human progress with a continued progress of technology. I also am grateful for the love and support that I have received from my mother (Dr. Mrs. Prajkta Mulay), my father (Dr. Pradeep Mulay), and my brother (Dr. Preshit Mulay) without whom it would not have been possible to accomplish authoring three volumes in three consecutive years, 2014, 2015, and 2016. I am very thankful to the Business Expert Press for bearing the costs of publishing this volume. I would fall short if I do not acknowledge the guidance that I have received from Professor Ravi Batra, without whom I would not have mastered a highly complicated and dynamic subject of macroeconomics. I extend my gratitude to Stephen Willis for authoring an introductory Foreword to this volume. I would also extend my gratitude to Yin Li for permitting to use his research in Chapter 3 of this volume. I will also like to acknowledge the encouragement that I received from Joel Claypool in completing this volume.

I dedicate this volume to the entire humanity on this planet, with a hope that we can collaborate in order to hasten the arrival of a new crimson dawn on the eastern horizon and put an end to the unnecessary suffering caused by poverty and destitution with a rapid technological progress. I am optimistic that this volume would lead to the dawn of a new golden age of high prosperity and growth for every human being with a productive utilization of semiconductor technology. Last, but not the least, I would also like to extend my gratitude to all my family members, friends, and teachers who have had an immensely important role to play in shaping up my personality and career. It would not have been possible for me to achieve it without their enriching contributions to my life.

Apek Mulay
July 2016

CHAPTER 1

The Magic of Moore's Law on Knowledge-based Economy

Introduction

The benefits of Moore's law to human progress can be traced to a universal value an end user in form of transistors. The more the number of transistors on an electronic circuitry, the greater is the functionality of the product the consumers can buy. In this way, the number of transistors translates into system functionality. Therefore, by cramming more transistors on an integrated circuit (IC), it is possible to not only add value to the final product but, by means of mass production, to also minimize or reduce the costs of production. In this way, Moore's law has been able to offer a lot of value to the semiconductor industry by offering a higher value to consumers and at the same time reducing the costs for the manufacturers. Thereby, it has contributed to every new innovation in the consumer electronics and provided a profitable business model for the semiconductor industry.

A Brief History of Technological Developments in Economy Preventing Demise of Moore's Law

Moore's law has served as an important benchmark for the development of microelectronics and information processing during the last five decades. During these five decades, the technical requirements of optimal chip manufacturing costs have been extended to include the processor performance, economics of computing, as well as economic development of society. The 50 years of progress of the semiconductor industry based on the progress of Moore's law has been associated with rapid changes in information processing technologies. A rapid growth in chip complexity accompanied by "*cramming more components onto integrated circuits*" has rapidly increased the productivity, processing speed, etc. through the introduction of innovations contributing to the rapid growth of the knowledge-based economy.

In his 1965 paper, Gordon Moore notes that the total cost of making a particular system function must be minimized. One way of achieving this would be to mass-produce the chips so that the engineering costs could be amortized over many identical chips. Another way would be to develop flexible design techniques that could be used for many different chips. In other words, the design focus has to be either on making high volumes of a single function or on making designs that could be reused for many different chips. The approach to focus the design on making high volumes of a single function resulted in the exponential growth of the memory market. The invention of the microprocessor combined the benefits of both high-volume manufacturing and reuse of design work in high-volume multifunctional chips. As the universal microprocessors made the application developers pay for most of the design costs, the costs of semiconductor manufacturing dropped radically as much of the difficulty and cost of designing complex systems was off-loaded to system and software designers. The development of the calculator and the advent of semiconductor memory devices in the mid-1960s helped generate more demand for semiconductor products, sustaining the progress of Moore's law during that decade.

The period from 1950 to 1970 is considered to be a golden era of free market capitalism in the United States because during these decades the wages of the workforce caught up with the productivity of the workforce. Hence, it was not surprising that the ICs introduced during the period 1959 to 1975 followed the predicted trend of Moore's law as per his 1965 paper relatively well. In 1975, Intel introduced its first general purpose 8080 processor that started the personal computer (PC) revolution. The macroeconomic changes that happened in the U.S. economy after 1970, especially after 1980, shifted the focus of the economy to supply-side economics, and the United States lost the golden era of free market capitalism. As a result of macroeconomic policies enacted during the tenure of Ronald Reagan's presidency, a major economic crisis hit in 1984–1985, and since then, macroeconomic policies have resulted in boom-and-bust cycles that have plagued the global economy to date. Preparing for the rapid expansion of markets, Intel Inc. licensed the 80286 microprocessor to other manufacturers, including AMD, Fujitsu, Siemens, and IBM. There was a big boom in 1983, which continued into the middle of 1984—and then the semiconductor world collapsed in late 1984 and 1985. The resulting crisis caused Intel to lay off its workforce and shut down several factories. Hence a policy of merely giving tax cuts to businesses does not revive the economy but may hurt it further when businesses have to lay off their workforce, and the consequences observed in 1984–85 of Reagan's 1981 tax cuts is evidence of the same.

In the mid-1980s, just when no one seemed to be able to make a profit, the IBM PC and Microsoft saved the day. After the great economic crisis of 1987, China's economy also opened up, and the United States started offshoring manufacturing to China as Japan's economy crashed in 1989 because of the Plaza Accord. Since the Intel 80286 processors that were shipped in 1982, microprocessors have utilized parallel processing in many alternative forms. By parallelism, more operations can be accomplished within a time unit. Since the mid-1990s, microprocessor architectures have increasingly relied on program compilers that detect and optimize parallelism in the source code programs. Indeed, the innovations in compiler technology have been a main driver in processing power improvements and not just the cramming of components on the IC. However, the development of software that compiled computer programs into machine code started to add to the growth in productivity. Thus in the mid-1990s, the Internet and World Wide Web (WWW) exploded the hard disk and memory market and created the need for new processor architectures (that were able to handle images, sound, and video), which helped sustain the progress of Moore's law. However, as a result of the focus of the economy only on the supply side since the 1980s, there was a major economic crisis at the threshold of the new millennium.

During the last four decades, the microprocessor architectures have changed considerably. Starting with Intel's 486 processor series, so-called cache memory began to be included on the same silicon die as the processor. Processor chips, therefore, became a combination of processors and memory. As memory chips have a considerably higher density of transistors than microprocessor chips, this combination of memory with processors led to a rapid increase in the number of transistors on such integrated processor chips. Since late 1999, Intel has not included transistor counts in its processor summaries. In October 1999, Intel Pentium III Xeon and Mobile Pentium III processors had some 28 million transistors. In July 2001, Pentium 4 had about 42 million transistors. Most of these transistors were cache memory. In this way, the transistor counts on microprocessors have increased very rapidly because they have closed their earlier gap with memory chips. Indeed, it seems that Intel is again in the memory business. This is how the progress of Moore's law has been cramming more and more components on an IC. However, this growth has been unsustainable, and eventually, in 2008, the subprime crisis due to the focus on supply-side economics nearly collapsed the U.S. economy.

After the subprime crisis of 2008, the global demand for smartphones has been driving the growth of the semiconductor industry and the progress of Moore's law. While the demand for laptops and PCs has started to slow down, there has been an exponential growth in smartphones around the globe. While Original Equipment Manufacturers (OEMs) like Apple Inc. have become very cash rich with the exploding growth of smartphones, countries like India have been running huge trade deficits owing to the absence of any domestically manufactured smartphones to cater to the need of its ever-growing population. In addition, there has been a decrease in demand for Intel Processors due to reduced demand for PCs and laptops, but there has been a rise in the demand for ARM processors to be used in smartphones. This has also forced Intel Inc. to open manufacturing even to its competitors in order to let them use Intel's excess manufacturing capacity, and Intel Inc. has been going on an acquisition spree to compete in the wireless business.

During its history, the semiconductor industry has often hit the speed limit for continuing the technological progress of Moore's law. The invention of the digital clock and the calculator helped sustain the progress of Moore's law in mid-1960s. The mini- and mainframe computer industry helped sustain the progress of Moore's law during the 1970s. As mentioned before, in the mid-1980s, just when no one seemed to be able to make a profit, the IBM PC and Microsoft saved the day. Similarly, It was the advent of Internet and WWW which exploded the hard disk and memory market. This invention created a demand for new processor architectures that were able to handle images, sound and video. Since the millennium, the explosion in demand for cell phones and smartphones has helped sustain the progress of Moore's law. Today, the resulting economic disparity resulting from the focus of macroeconomic policies on supply-side economics has resulted in a failure of central bank policies in stimulating domestic economic demand. This has created another stock market bubble not only in the U.S. economy but in the global economy. Now, the semiconductor industry is banking on the Internet of Things (IoT) to generate the next wave of demand. Hence, for Moore's law to be able to continue benefitting the global economy and usher in an IoT revolution, the focus should be to raise the economic demand in proportion to the supply of the number of transistors, and future chapters will envision how to make it possible through free market economic policies.

The Virtuous Cycle of Semiconductor Industry

As clearly stated in the executive summary of International Technology Roadmap for Semiconductors (ITRS), "a basic premise of the Roadmap has been that continued scaling of electronics would further reduce the cost per function and promote market-growth for integrated circuits." Since the observation made by Gordon Moore as early as 1965 until today, the semiconductor industry has made use of Moore's law as a guide to its progress. Hence, the technological roadmap of ITRS can be traced back to 1965, when Gordon Moore made an observation that the number of transistors would keep on growing exponentially on an IC.

When the number of components such as transistors, bits, etc. on an IC increases, the total chip size has to be contained within practical and affordable limits. In today's ICs, the typical size of DRAM is less than 145 sq. mm., and the typical size of a microprocessor unit (MPU) is approximately 310 sq. mm. This can be achieved by a continuous downscaling of the critical dimensions in an IC. Moore's law could be expressed as a linear shrink of dimensions by a factor of 0.7 every 2 years, where "critical dimension" is understood as "half pitch," as defined in the ITRS roadmap for semiconductors.

This growth in the supply of transistors has greatly enhanced the productivity of modern ICs and consumer electronics. Today, approximately 3 billion people carry smartphones in their pockets. Each of the handheld smartphones is more powerful than a room-size supercomputer from the 1980s or even the computers needed to launch Apollo 11 to the Moon in 1969. As a rule of thumb, when smaller transistors are more tightly packed on an IC, there is a boost to performance of the chip and a reduction in its cost. An example of performance gains achieved by the semiconductor industry can be understood from the fact that today's Intel Skylake processor contains around 1.75 billion transistors. Approximately half a million of these would fit inside a single transistor of Intel 4004 MPU in 1971. The presence of half a million transistors also delivers 400,000 times as much computing power as a single transistor in 1971.

As the performance and productivity of ICs started to grow, the supply of consumer electronics with higher performance also started to grow. There was always a rising consumer demand for advanced electronic gadgets, and that kept the demand for consumer electronics high enough to call for further investments to drive the progress of Moore's law. Thus, the supply of goods called for more demand and thereby kept the virtuous cycle of the semiconductor industry sustaining the progress of Moore's law. While the consumers benefited from the advancements in the latest and greatest electronic gadgets, the producers benefited from the consumption of manufactured electronics, thereby keeping this economic cycle of supply driving demand and demand further driving more supply in constant motion. This became the virtuous cycle of the semiconductor industry leading to the establishment of a knowledge-based economy.

The virtuous cycle of semiconductors exists because of the better performance-to-cost ratio of products, which has resulted in an exponential growth of the semiconductor market. The predictability of a good Return on Investments (RoI) resulted in a high degree of confidence shared by different semiconductor industry players that enabled the progress of Moore's law and brought the much expected benefits for the semiconductor industry.

Progress of Other Industries Related to Semiconductor Industry

The continued progress of Moore's law has resulted in a lot of investments in the economy. The progress of the semiconductor manufacturing process involves not just physics but also chemistry of different chemicals that would be used in the semiconductor manufacturing process. Besides, consumer electronics started finding applications in day-to-day use for consumers, which are not restricted to the use of automobiles, aircrafts, home appliances, kitchenware, etc. Along with an exponential growth of various applications making use of semiconductors, there was also an exponential growth of the demand for ICs. In this way, progress of the semiconductor industry resulting from the continuous progress of Moore's law has also resulted in the growth of other industries catering to the progress of today's knowledge-based economy. Thus did the semiconductor industry become a principal driver for the economic growth of high tech and innovation.

The last 50 years of rapid progress of Moore's law ushered in the third industrial revolution, also known as the "Digital Revolution," in the global economy. The progress of the semiconductor industry led to the adoption and proliferation of digital computers and digital record keeping that continues till date. It was the spectacular progress of the semiconductor industry driven by the progress of Moore's law that resulted in the beginning of the Information Age. It would not have been possible to achieve the third industrial revolution without mass production and widespread use of technologies like computer, digital cellular phone, and Internet based on digital logic circuits. The rapid growth in the number of cell phone users worldwide is evidence of the magic of Moore's law. The number of cell phone users grew from 11.2 million in 1980 to cross the 4-billion mark by 2010. Also, the number of Internet users grew from 2.8 million in 1990 to 1.8 billion users by 2010. This rapid growth in the number of users connected through the spread of Internet is leading to the fourth industrial revolution in the form of IoT. Thus, the progress of Moore's law led to the development of transmission technologies like computer networking, the Internet, and digital broadcasting, which also led to an exponential growth and social penetration of 3G phones along with new consumer electronic gadgets providing ubiquitous entertainment, communications, and online connectivity. The present progress toward 4G and 5G penetration is only possible as long as consumer demand keeps growing in the global economy in order to sustain a demand for more technological advancements.

Socioeconomic Impact Resulting From the Progress of Moore's Law

As Moore's law started to progress on the physical front, it resulted in mass production of consumer electronics, which made them affordable. Thus, things that were once considered to be a luxury became a necessity because of rapid technological progress, which resulted from the progress of Moore's law. This progress led to the birth of a knowledge-based economy, resulting in greater interconnectedness, easier communication, and exposure to a vast amount of information that in the past could be easily suppressed by totalitarian regimes.

In his 2011 volume, *Physics of the Future: How Science Will Shape Human Destiny and Our Daily Lives by year 2100,* author *Michio Kaku* points to a long history of failed predictions against progress of science and technology, and considers it to be very dangerous to bet against the future. He mentions that the failure of the Soviet coup in 1991 was due to the presence of technology like fax machines and computers, which exposed the information that was once classified by the Soviet Communists. Realizing the importance of technology, many world governments could pass laws to restrict the use of technology in order to retain their control over the masses. But any such attempts are bound to fail, and scientific progress will continue to take humanity toward a crimson dawn of a new golden age and opportunity. The Arab spring revolutions against totalitarian regimes were also enabled by social networking as well as the use of smartphone technology.

Although WWW has been able to achieve a greater economic impact and has helped globalization and outsourcing, the absence of proper macroeconomic policies has resulted in this economic impact turning out to be very counterproductive. Hence, if Moore's law has to continue on its path of progress to sustain the socioeconomic impacts from the progress of digital technology, a productive use of technology based on sound macroeconomic policies is mandatory. This is evident from the fact that although digital technology provided e-commerce businesses with access to a much larger market, small companies did get access to a much larger market, but the absence of good macroeconomic policies is resulting in monopolization of markets by a few big players, thereby causing major bankruptcies for many small businesses and lack of entry into the market for many new businesses.

Although digital technologies have significantly increased the productivity and performance of businesses, it also came with a drop in the productivity of company employees due to the pervasive use of portable digital devices as well as use of social networks, personal emails, instant messaging, computer games, etc. on their office computers. As long as accountability does not come along with the ability to use technological productivity, such an abuse is going to continue. Hence, there have to be better metrics of measurement of rapid performance with the progress of technology. In that regard, *mass capitalism* provides a very good alternative as it provides a stake in the success of the business, by making every employee a part-owner in business. This in itself empowers employees to be more productive at their jobs as low productivity will hurt their own paycheck.

Another socioeconomic impact of the progress of Moore's law was the advent of the Internet, especially WWW, in the 1990s, which provided new avenues for communication and information sharing. This took freedom of speech to a whole new level. Social networking sites like LinkedIn, Facebook, Twitter, etc. provided individuals and organizations with alternative to publish on any topic, and get a global readership at a fractional cost, when compared with communications technologies of the past. It led to the advent of large co-operative projects like open-source projects, SETI@home, etc. Here, I make a forecast that this continued progress of technology will result in the formation of more consumer cooperatives and transform the existing business models in global economy to a more consumer-centric business model, resulting in healthy co-operative interaction between the producers and the consumers.

Every progress in society comes through clashes and cohesion. Hence, along with the positive contributions of technology also comes its abuse. Today, we find pornographic material is readily available to minors through the use of Internet. Additionally, terrorist organizations like ISIS are actively recruiting youth through the Internet. Hence, there is a threat of danger with the use of the Internet. These could be avoided through proper laws regulating the use of the Internet and by creating a healthy economy that provides an equal and fair opportunity to every individual in society to utilize his or her talents toward the best interest of humanity.

A Brief Evolution of Different Types of Semiconductor Companies that Have Profoundly been Shaped by the Progress of Moore's Law

The 50 years of progress of Moore's law has resulted in a rapid transformation of the global semiconductor industry. While the scope of discussion of this section is vast, we shall focus our analysis by taking an example of those semiconductor companies whose business models have been transformed by a rapid progress of Moore's law. In this process, we shall also analyze the relative contributions of these companies in creating jobs in the economy as well as the revenue generated from profitability of operations.

While the progress of Moore's law has resulted in a transformation of the global semiconductor industry from a few Integrated Device Manufacturers (IDMs) to several fabless semiconductor companies, the key driver of this trend has been the exponentially rising costs of establishing a state-of-the-art semiconductor foundry. Today, it costs approximately $10 billion to construct a state-of-the-art semiconductor foundry. Considering depreciation over a 5-year duration, the costs of establishing a $10 billion foundry is about $50 per second. In addition to this cost, there is an added cost for paying the highly qualified engineering staff and well-trained managerial staff. In addition to these costs, the use of silicon wafers and chemicals to manufacture the electronics is a continuous process. On average, a foundry manufactures approximately 50,000 wafers per month.

When Gordon Moore first made his famous observation in 1965, the costs of establishing a state-of-the-art foundry were not in billions. At that time, it was possible for a few players to own the design, manufacture, assembling, as well as testing facilities. As the cost of ownership of a foundry was low, there were no semiconductor companies that did not own a fab until 1980. Hence, the prevalent business model of semiconductor industry until 1980 was the IDM business model. One example of such IDM is Intel Inc., which is one of the few IDMs still in existence today. These IDMs, which had excess capacity, would often offer to do manufacturing for other semiconductor companies that had smaller fabs or did not have sufficient manufacturing capacity to meet their customer needs. This was beneficial also to the manufacturing foundries as their excess capacity was used up, and they made good revenue by means of maximum utilization of their manufacturing capacity. Hence, for a foundry to remain profitable, it had to make maximum utilization of its manufacturing capacity and keep its tools in operation 24 × 7.

In this way, there existed collaboration between different semiconductor foundries in order to even out their manufacturing capacities. Semiconductor companies would get their wafers manufactured even from a competitor's foundry (if there was a surplus capacity with the competitor). However, things started to change in the mid-1980s when companies like Xilinx realized that they do not need to own a foundry but could just manufacture wafers using other foundries and sell the products to their customers. Such companies were called fabless semiconductor companies. The fabless business model got a big boost with the establishment of the Taiwan Semiconductor Manufacturing Company (TSMC) as the first pure-play semiconductor foundry that manufactured wafers for several fabless semiconductor companies. Today, TSMC is one of the most dominant and most profitable pure-play semiconductor foundries, and Qualcomm Inc. is one of the most profitable fabless semiconductor companies.

The establishment of TSMC helped bring about a fabless revolution in the semiconductor industry as many Silicon Valley venture capitalists funded several fabless businesses owing to lower costs of operation from offshoring manufacturing to TSMC. However, as technology continued to advance with the progress of Moore's law, IDMs like Texas Instruments Inc. and Advanced Micro Devices (AMD) Inc. realized that it was too expensive to own a state-of-the-art foundry, and hence, AMD became fabless and AMD Inc. sold its fabs to an investment consortium, which later became what is today *GlobalFoundries*. However, *Texas Instruments Inc.* purchased external capacity for advanced semiconductor manufacturing from offshore foundries like TSMC, SMIC (Semiconductor Manufacturing International Corporation), Chartered, etc., but it retained many of its original foundries for manufacturing its products. Such companies like *Texas Instruments Inc.* became fab-lite semiconductor company. Let us compare the revenues over the years for *Intel Inc., Texas Instruments Inc., Qualcomm Inc.,* and TSMC since the 2008 financial crisis to have one example each of IDM, fab-lite, fabless, and pure-play foundry.

Table 1.1 *Annual revenue from 2008 to 2015 for Intel Inc., Texas Instruments Inc., Qualcomm Inc. and TSMC*

Semiconductor Company Name and Type of Semiconductor Company	2008 Annual Revenue (in Billions)	2009 Annual Revenue (in Billions)	2010 Annual Revenue (in Billions)	2011 Annual Revenue (in Billions)	2012 Annual Revenue (in Billions)	2013 Annual Revenue (in Billions)	2014 Annual Revenue (in Billions)	2015 Annual Revenue (in Billions)
Intel Inc. [1] (IDM)	37.5	35.13	43.6	54.2	53.3	52.7	55.9	55.4
Texas Instruments Inc. [2] (Fab-lite)	12.5	10.43	13.97	13.74	12.83	12.21	13.0	13.0
Qualcomm Inc. [3] (Fabless)	11.13	10.39	10.98	14.96	19.12	24.87	26.49	25.28
TSMC[4] (Pure-Play Semiconductor Foundry)	10.56	9.56	13.32	13.28	15.64	18.43	23.54	26.08

Source: [1]https://newsroom.intel.com/news-releases/

[2]http://www.ti.com/corp/docs/investor_relations/financial_summary_data.html

[3]http://investor.qualcomm.com/annuals-proxies.cfm

[4]http://www.tsmc.com/english/investorRelations/financial_reports.htm

Conclusion

The magic of Moore's law on the progress of the knowledge-based economy has been on democratization of information and communication, thereby gradually empowering the masses to influence markets, politics, and culture. 50 years of progress of Moore's law was not the result of an individual effort but of a collective effort by a global consortium of semiconductor companies, academia, as well as government focused on meeting the roadmap of the semiconductor industry associated with the progress of Moore's law. If a similar focus is maintained by the global consortium along with a focus on local economic development in order to boost the economic demand at the local level with the solutions that I have proposed in this volume, the true magic of Moore's law will lift the human society from an abyss to a new crimson dawn of broader economic progress. This factuality is as glazy, as graceful, as glamorous, and as colorful as the rising crimson sun on the eastern horizon bringing about an end to the gloomy dark night.

Suggested Readings

[1] Wolfgang Arden, Brillouet Michael, Cogez Patrick, Graef Mart, Huizing Bert, Mahnkopf Reinhard, Pelka Joachim, Pfeiffer Jens-Uwe, Rouzaud Andre, Tartagni Marco, Chris Van Hoof, Wagner Joachim, "*Towards a More-than-Moore Roadmap*", Report from the CATRENE Scientific Community. November 8, 2011.

[2] Wikipedia, "*Digital Revolution*". https://en.wikipedia.org/wiki/Digital _Revolution

[3] Mulay, Apek, *Mass Capitalism: A Blueprint for Economic Revival*, Book Publishers Network, Bothell, WA, 2014.

[4] Mulay, Apek, *Sustaining Moore's Law: Uncertainty Leading to a Certainty of IoT Revolution*, Morgan & Claypool Publishers, San Rafael,CA, 2015.

[5] Sarkar, Prabhat Ranjan, *PROUT in a Nutshell*, Ananda Marga Publications, Kolkata, India, 1959.

[6] Tuomi, Ilkka, '*The lives and death of Moore's law*', First Monday, Vol.7, No. 11, November 4, 2002. http://firstmonday.org/ojs/index.php/fm/article/view /1000/921

CHAPTER 2

Return on Investments
With Moore's Law

Introduction

The 50 years of progress of the semiconductor industry has been propelled by the ability to drive the progress of Moore's law toward achieving a better return on investments (RoI). The first company to shrink the dimensions of transistor to achieve the next technological node was the first to capture the market share for the latest and greatest products. In this way, progress of Moore's law not only led to a rapid growth in productivity by means of technological growth but also resulted in a better RoI with growth in the market share for most advanced products. The improved RoI thereby attracted more investments into the economy, leading to a more productive utilization of wealth.

A Collaborative Business Model to Ensure a Good RoI

In general, the RoI on any project depends on the health of a macroeconomy. When a huge investment is required for a business, it limits the entry to only a select few who have a lot of money to invest. In such a scenario, it results in a lack of competition and lack of free markets, causing a few big businesses to monopolize the marketplace based on their strength of capital. Now, if new entrants cannot enter the marketplace, not only does it result in monopoly of a few but also puts barriers for new innovations to enter the marketplace. This is because most innovations come from small businesses.

In Chapter 5 entitled "Fabless versus Integrated Device Manufacturer," I have provided a comparison of two prevalent business models in global semiconductor industry, viz., fabless-foundry business model and Integrated Device Manufacturer (IDM) business model. I have also put forth a new business model that ensures better collaboration and broader prosperity in the economy. The proposed new business model takes into consideration all the advantages of both fabless and IDM business models on the macroeconomic level and discards their macroeconomic disadvantages. When there are fewer barriers for entry into the marketplace and more prosperity for any business by means of steady growth in the consumer demand, it results in more innovations in the economy and better chances of small businesses to prosper. This kind of collaboration would play an important role in ensuring a good RoI for further progress of Moore's law.

Over the last half a century of progress of Moore's law, as the number of components (i.e., transistors, bits) per chip increased, the total chip size has to be contained within practical and affordable limits (typical chip size was lower than 145 mm^2 for dynamic random access memories (DRAMs) and lower than 310 mm^2 for microprocessors). This can be achieved by a continuous downscaling of the critical dimensions on the integrated circuit. As a consequence of this trend, the miniaturization of circuits by scaling down of the transistor has been the principal driver for the semiconductor technology roadmap for the last half a century. Due to its ability to decrease the cost per elementary function dramatically, the global semiconductor industry has over the years reached annual revenue close to $300 billion. This achievement of the semiconductor business has exceeded the achievement of several other technology sectors such as telecommunications, automotives, consumer electronics, etc., and has enabled the emergence of entirely new markets like personal computers (PCs), laptops, tablets, smartphones, etc.

The wide applicability of semiconductor technology in numerous applications also has had a widespread impact on many other industries because of considerable reduction in cost per function. With the progress of Moore's law, it has become possible to manufacture more and more transistors on an integrated circuit (IC), which has reduced the cost per function on an IC because the addition of every transistor corresponds to an increase in the performance with added functionality as well as reduction in cost per added function. However, it should be noted that

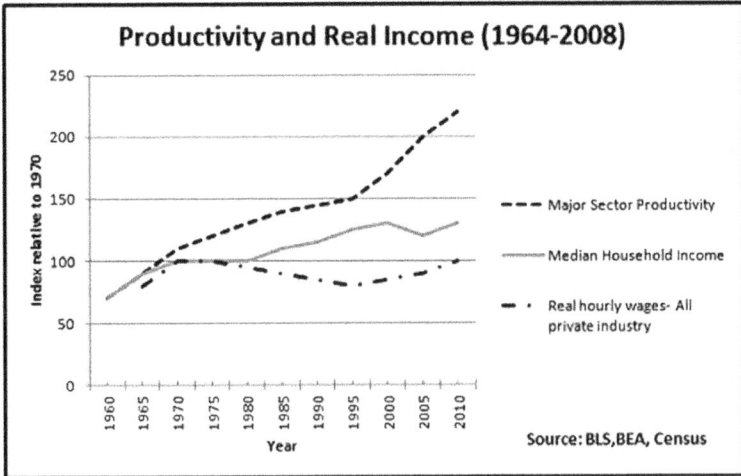

Figure 2.1 *The wage–productivity gap in the U.S. economy from 1964 to 2008*

Source: Mass Capitalism: A Blueprint for Economic Revival.

this long-term deflationary effect of semiconductors may not have been fully accounted for in statistics and econometrics. As an example, the decline in price per bit has been stunning over the years of progress of Moore's law. In 1954, 5 years before the integrated circuit was invented, the average selling price of a transistor was U.S. $5.52. Fifty years later, in 2004, this had dropped to a billionth of a dollar. A year later in 2005 the cost per bit of DRAM is an astounding one nanodollar (one billionth of a dollar).

Thus, in order to ensure a continuous growth in productivity from technological advancements, it has become critical to make necessary reforms in the existing business models of the semiconductor industry alongwith pursuing some major macroeconomic reforms to ensure that there are good RoI for more investments to arrive in the economy.

As we can observe from Figures 2.1 and 2.2, the real wages have failed to keep up with productivity in the overall U.S. economy, and the semi-conductor industry is no exception to this trend. The productivity of American workers has been consistently increasing. However, the average household median income has not increased at the rate at which produc-tivity has increased. The real hourly wages have remained fairly constant.

Labor Productivity, Employment and Compensation Trends in Semiconductors and
Electronic Components
Note: Productivity, employment and compensation are presented here as indexes that represent their values at each year relative to the base year (1997)

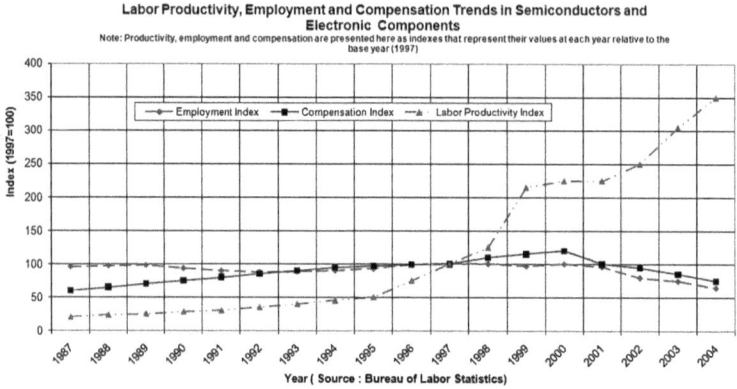

Figure 2.2 Labor productivity, employment, and compensation trends in the U.S. semiconductor industry from 1987 to 2004

Source: Mass Capitalism: A Blueprint for Economic Revival.

The United States needs to reform its current economic model so that wages keep track with the productivity of workers. When wages catch up with productivity, supply catches up with demand, and hence, there is no unproductive utilization of wealth in an economy. This is because when any additional investment arrives into the economy, it is bound to generate a good RoI. However, when supply exceeds demand, without the creation of new debt in the economy, it is impossible for the existing production to get consumed that leads to an unproductive utilization of wealth in an economy.

In the chapter "The Macroeconomics of 450 mm diameter Silicon Wafers" of my volume *Sustaining Moore's Law* (2015), I have explained in-depth how an unproductive utilization of wealth results in recessions and depressions in an economy; I will summarize this aspect in the following few paragraphs. The global semiconductor industry has been constantly increasing the diameter of the silicon wafers it uses in order to reduce its manufacturing costs through mass production. The larger the diameter of wafers, the more is the real estate of silicon that is available for manufacturing. The increasing process complexities in nanoscale engineering add to silicon manufacturing costs. However, if the percentage increase in the manufacturing costs per wafer due to advancements in technology is smaller than the percentage increase in revenue due to the larger real estate of silicon, then the semiconductor manufacturing business becomes profitable.

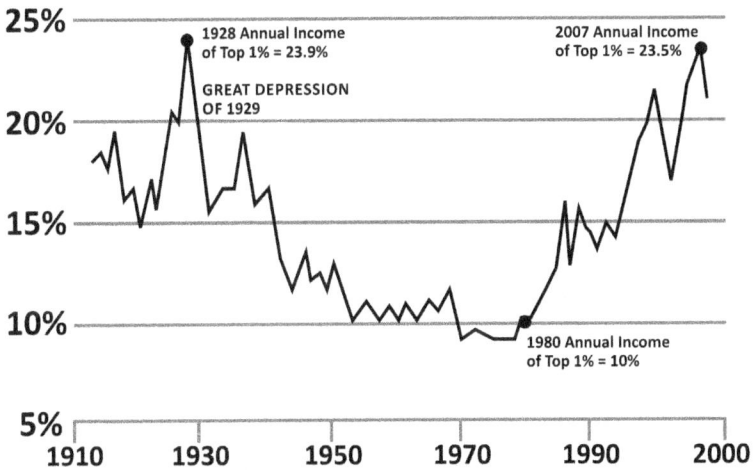

Figure 2.3 *Annual income of richest 1 percent of population from 1910 to 2010. When the disparity has increased such that just 1 percent earns close to 24 percent of annual income in the economy, the economy goes into a depression*

Source: Mass Capitalism: A Blueprint for Economic Revival.

At present, the semiconductor industry is widely making use of 300 mm diameter silicon wafers, and there is some progress toward 450 mm diameter wafers, but major players like Intel, TSMC, Samsung, etc. are delaying their investments for 450 mm diameter wafers due to significantly high manufacturing costs of semiconductor processing tools and lower expected RoI. The major players in this business do not expect to reap significant returns from their huge capital investments, which gives rise to questions as to whether mass production of 450 mm diameter wafers would become a reality anytime in the near future.

On the macroeconomic side of the U.S. economy, the purchasing power of majority of the consumers has shrunk because of the transformation of the economy from a free market enterprise to monopoly capitalism. As a result, there is a growing gap between the wages and the productivity of employees in the U.S. and global economy, which is resulting in a loss of economic balance. As demonstrated in Figure 2.3 above, this gap has increased economic disparity such that it has fueled a debate resulting from an economic disparity between the top 1 percent and remaining 99 percent. When capitalism is reformed to a free market enterprise, which of course works for all citizens in an economy, it would usher in an economic democracy. As it would work for all citizens, monopoly capitalism will become *mass capitalism*.

In order to sustain the progress of semiconductor industry which has been driven by the relentless progress of Moore's law, macroeconomic reforms have become critical to allow semiconductor companies to justify their ever-increasing capital-intensive investments for transitioning to 450 mm diameter wafers. By establishing free markets, supply and demand of electronic goods would grow in proportion, thereby resulting in a balanced economic growth, low income taxes on individuals, higher investments, increased motivation for employees to work hard, and the growth of the overall economy. These free market reforms seem to be the only path forward for the global semiconductor industry to ensure its sustainability for transition to 450 mm diameter silicon wafers.

Hence, there should be an approach to achieving a collaborative ecosystem where resources could be shared in such a way that the model is symbiotic or mutually beneficial. Obviously, building a capital-intensive infrastructure for peak loads becomes wasteful when the load is not at its peak, so the new business model should enable the optimum utilization of an infrastructure service for demand spikes, which can level out the costs. Only a three-tier business model as presented in subsequent chapters will be able to address the problem of growing costs of infrastructure alongwith preserving innovations in the economy.

To meet the above-mentioned requirements in a capital-intensive business, I propose a three-tier business model for the semiconductor industry as well as for the Internet of Things (IoT) to achieve a maximum utilization and rational distribution of resources in an economy to sustain the progress of Moore's law as well as to achieve success of the fourth industrial revolution in the form of IoT. The lack of this three-tier business model not only brings about the demise of Moore's law due to economics but even today's cloud service providers are not able to offer their services to customers at lower costs as compared to the earlier generations in the progress of Moore's law. Let me explain this with an example for the Infrastructure as a Service (IaaS). IaaS is a form of cloud computing that provides virtualized computing resources over the Internet. IaaS is one of three main categories of cloud computing services, alongside Software as a Service (SaaS) and Platform as a Service (PaaS). Leading IaaS providers include Amazon Web Services (AWS), Windows Azure, Google Compute Engine, Rackspace Open Cloud, and IBM Smart Cloud Enterprise.

Back in 2006, AWS based the unit cost on a single Xeon core processor running at 1.7 GHz. From that base, prices could go up depending on myriad factors, including memory needs and the term of contract, 3 years being the longest period. Amazon updates its model over time based on newer processors that it integrates on its servers based on progress of Moore's law. Given the improvements in processor performance and storage capacity per drive, AWS customers should expect their prices to continually fall. In fact, the U.S. Department of Energy, in a recent report comparing the cost of the government's in-house supercomputing centers to commercial cloud services, concluded that Amazon pricing isn't keeping pace with Moore's law. This conclusion was arrived at based on the fact that typical computation offering in Amazon has fallen only 18 percent in 5 years, which translates into a compound annual improvement of roughly 4 percent. However, the number of cores available in a typical AWS server has increased 6 to 12 times over the same period with modest increase in costs. The root cause for this problem is the lack of a collaborative business model based on the free market theory of *mass capitalism* in Web services domain for the cloud services providers.

Milestones Achieved Due to High RoI With the Progress of Moore's Law

The doubling of power and halving of price that Moore noticed has continued apace for the last 50 years. Although there exist theoretical limits, due to physics, regarding how long shrinking of transistor dimensions could continue, these limits could be breached by the innovative human mind if quantum computing becomes practically applicable. For an individual user, progress of Moore's law means that the newly manufactured gadgets are able to do twice as many new, innovative, and unexpected things than before. This demand for the latest and greatest electronic gadgets has to be made sustainable. If consumers have to go into a huge debt to buy these latest gadgets then the economic system will lead to a much earlier demise of Moore's law as will be explained in subsequent chapters. However, when consumers buy the most advanced electronic gadgets through growth in their real wages in proportion to their grow-ing productivity, the demand is sustainable and technological progress of Moore's law can be sustained as long as possible.

The 50 years of progress of Moore's law has achieved significant RoI and reached great milestones. Just 10 years ago, most pessimists had not even expected or believed that people today would carry around with them hundreds or thousands or tens of thousands of their favorite songs in portable devices, which could be smaller than a cigarette pack. Nei-ther did many realize the democratization of publishing business due to 50 years of progress of Moore's law. Nobody would have believed that the cost of software and hardware needed to publish or broadcast their own writings or videos online would drop so low and become so easy to use that anyone could do it with their own blogs, social networks as well as professional networks. Similarly, Moore's law has also played an important role by ushering in the electronic commerce business and made online shopping a significant percentage of retail commerce, leading to a growth of new businesses and expansion of markets for many small businesses.

Today, people routinely make use of laptop computers or pocket-sized devices to watch videos without DVDs, have platforms to upload their own videos online to share with others, etc. In this way, techno-logical progress achieved with the progress of Moore's law has democ-ratized innovation. Thanks to the progress of Moore's law that millions of people today routinely make telephone or videophone calls from PCs or by means of downloading various applications like WhatsApp, etc. onto their smartphones. Similarly, today mobile phones are used primar-ily for text messaging and new cars are now equipped with tracking tools that map its co-ordinates road as well as guide the driver anywhere she or he wishes to go. All these numerous-to-mention have become possible because of a rapid progress of Moore's law over years. The addition of exponential number of transistors from the progress of Moore's law have enabled modern electronic gadgets to perform functions which we had expected out them.

The 50 years of progress of Moore's law has resulted in the manufac-ture of new things, creation of new opportunities, and new competitors in the business. Some old companies evolved and died and new ones arose. If this progress of Moore's law could be sustained by restoring free markets, we are going to witness a lot more changes happening in the economy. This progress can only be sustained by ensuring a good RoI and that is possible only by ensuring that consumers' purchasing power never goes down. Crony capitalism has not made it possible to continuously increase the purchasing power of the people, because economic power is concentrated in the hands of a few. Hence, RoI is diminishing and so the progress of Moore's law is now becoming unsustainable. However, when free market economic reforms are carried out in an economy based on the theory of *mass capitalism*, people's income will have an upward trend and their purchasing power will continuously increase. This will increase the real economic demand, and hence, the progress of Moore's law would become not only sustainable but also very profitable.

RoI Constraints in the Bitcoin Mining Industry

In the chapter entitled "Should USD Be Restored to Gold Standard?" in my volume *Mass Capitalism* (2014), I briefly discussed the impacts of geopolitics on the Bitcoin mining industry where I stressed the importance of a balanced free market economy to increase the stability of any currency and improve the standard of living of domestic citizens. In recent years, Bitcoin mining industry has undergone massive changes. Presently, miners are hitting Moore's Wall where technology is the first problem and economics is the second problem.

Adding more and more transistors and building massive chips with billions of transistors certainly increases performance but cooling these chips also becomes troublesome and impractical. At the same time, efficiency becomes an even bigger problem. As an emerging field of IC design, Bitcoin mining *Application-Specific Integrated Circuits* (ASICs) have experienced a rapid evolution but technical challenges to Moore's law cannot be overcome by the world's foremost chip designers and foundries. ASICs differ from general purpose processors and a lot less money goes into the development and optimization of ASICs. When designs mature, they cannot be optimized further and hence ASIC design inevitably slows down. Besides, ASICs are not mass market chips, and hence, reverse engineering is seldom done on these designs to provide an in-depth analysis of the root cause of the problem.

On the economic front, the problem with Bitcoin mining is economics, resulting from an increased difficulty in Bitcoin mining, outstripping the costs for development. This is evident from the fact that the hash rate of the Bitcoin network has skyrocketed from around 1,000,000GH/s in 2013 to more than 200,000,000GH/s in 2014, briefly peaking at 231,138,370GH/s in late August 2014. In roughly the same period the difficulty shot up from about 65 million to 27,428,630,902 on August 31, 2014. The high difficulty can be partly attributed to more efficient and powerful ASICs, but in reality, they come from huge investments in this high-risk industry.

As a result of an industrial progress based on supply-side economic policies, technology cannot evolve to offer a similar RoI-like past due to the falling real economic demand. While thermals and efficiency pose a big technological challenge, the bigger challenge is an economic one. At a price of $500, Bitcoin miners were able to generate about $1.8m in revenue each day. If the price does not go up they could end up making even less. If it goes down, the miners could pull when they would keep running their hardware for a loss. Thereby, the RoI would further decrease when the operating expenses, cost of capital, and investments in next-generation hardware development keep increasing and prices keep falling. As this continues, small miners will no longer be competitive in future. Unless the problem of falling economic demand is addressed by restoring free markets based on the theory of *mass capitalism*, we would witness increasing mergers and acquisitions (M&As) resulting in monopoly capitalism in the Bitcoin mining industry, leading to further centralization and consolidation. Hence, a good macroeconomic policy is critical for the Bitcoin mining industry to remain competitive.

Conclusion

In general, RoI depends on the health of the macroeconomy, or the basic forces of supply and demand. If the total production in a nation is in balance with the total economic demand, the goods that are manufactured by industries and services that are offered have a ready market and adequate profits. However, if macroeconomic policies of a nation do not ensure a growth in economic demand with growth in supply of goods, then supply exceeds demand. When supply exceeds demand, there is an overproduction that leads to recession and layoffs at the manufacturing facility. This reduces RoI as well as further investments until the real economic demand catches up with the supply. In such cases, RoI could become mediocre and may even become negative. Thus, a good RoI with progress of Moore's law can only be assured by ensuring a free market economic policy, which drives economic demand in proportion to the supply, thereby ensuring profitability of any project.

Suggested Readings

[1] Whitman, Art, *"Does the Cloud Keep Pace with Moore's Law?"*, Information Week. February 27, 2012. http://www.informationweek.com/cloud/infrastructure-as-a-service/does-the-cloud-keep-pace-with-moores-law/d/d-id/1103033?

[2] Margaret, Rouse, Boisvert Michelle,*"Infrastructure as a Service (IaaS)"*, Tech Target. January 2015. http://searchcloudcomputing.techtarget.com/definition/Infrastructure-as-a-Service-IaaS

[3] Hajdarbegovic, Nermin, *"Why Bitcoin Mining Can No Longer Ignore Moore's Law"*. September 14, 2014. http://www.coindesk.com/bitcoin-mining-can-longer-ignore-moores-law/

[4] Crosbie, Vin, *"What Moore's Law Means to You?"*, ClickZ. January 23, 2009. https://www.clickz.com/clickz/column/1691994/what-moores-law-means-you

[5] Mulay, Apek, *Mass Capitalism: A Blueprint for Economic Revival*, Book Publishers Network, Bothell, WA, 2014.

[6] Mulay, Apek, *Sustaining Moore's Law: Uncertainty Leading to a Certainty of IoT Revolution*, Morgan & Claypool Publishers, San Rafael, CA, 2015.

CHAPTER 3

Impact of Moore's Law on the Transformation of Chinese Semiconductor Industry

Introduction

This volume is about the progress of semiconductor industry where the numbers of transistors on an integrated circuit have been doubling approximately every 2 years, a rate that has held strong for more than half a century. The nature of this exponential trend was first proposed by the Intel co-founder Gordon Moore in 1965. The name of the trend coined was "Moore's law," and its accuracy has proven to be a guiding factor for more than half a century of technological progress in the semiconductor industry to define its long-term planning and its ability to accurately set targets for R&D. An ignorance of common-sense macroeconomics in sustaining the progress of Moore's law has resulted in the transformation of the U.S. semiconductor industry over the years, eventually leading to the transformation of the U.S. economy from free market enterprise to crony capitalism.

In this chapter, we will take a look at the other side of the story where we will briefly analyze the transformation of the Chinese semiconductor industry over the years. We will try to look into the several factors that led to the rise of the Chinese economy due to a robust growth of its semiconductor industry. The factors leading to the rise of Chinese semiconductor industry have been identified based on the research report of *Yin Li*, entitled "From Classic Failures to Global Competitors: Business Organization and Economic Development in the Chinese Semiconductor Industry." However, we will also analyze the main reasons behind the economic crash of the Chinese economy in the summer of 2015, resulting in a sharp slowdown in all sectors of the Chinese economy including semiconductors. We will conclude this chapter by offering solutions for a bright future for the Chinese economy through a continued growth of its semiconductor industry.

Changes in Social Conditions Contributing to the Growth of Chinese Semiconductor Industry

The semiconductor industry is the foundation of knowledge-based economy of any nation. Every nation wants to have a robust semiconductor industry to drive innovations as well as to develop indigenous technology that would play a vital role in its national security. In Chapter 6 entitled "US Economic Boom to Economic Bust" of my volume *Mass Capitalism* (2014), I offered an elaborate discussion of how the United States has lost its economic dominance to China when it comes to the high-tech semiconductor manufacturing sector. It also becomes essential for us to understand how China was able to become a global manufacturing hub for semiconductors. This has also helped in the transformation of Chinese economy from communism to a state capitalism where the economic rights of the citizens have received some recognition and the semiconductor industry has played an important role in that regard. Semiconductor manufacturing industry is an extremely capital-intensive industry. Hence, it was not just the low labor costs in China that had convinced several global MNCs to move their manufacturing operations to China. The industrial policy makers in China have made great efforts to adopt the following three social conditions proposed by Professor William Lazonick for establishing an innovative enterprise such as "strategic control," "organizational integration," and "financial commitment." *Yin Li*'s research had identified these core principles to the success of innovative enterprises in the Chinese semiconductor industry. We will briefly discuss them and also try to understand why these policy-makers failed to ensure the establishment of a true free market economy in China, a failure that led to the crash of China's stock markets in the summer of 2015. We will conclude this chapter by trying to understand what reforms need to be adopted by China in order to ensure a sustainable progress of its knowledge-based economy by means of learning from its past mistakes.

In order to bring about macroeconomic reforms that would be essential to help the citizens as well as national economy, there have to be social institutions as well as stakeholders to achieve that success. When we have a stakeholder system, it empowers individuals as well as the overall organization to become responsible toward achieving a common goal. It gives a "strategic control" in the hands of the stakeholders, who would be responsible for making a decision that would directly impact allocation of resources to support innovative investment strategies. Investments in establishing a state-of-the-art semiconductor foundry involves a high fixed cost, which is approximately U.S. $10 billion. With such huge investments and with an expected accelerated depreciation of the state-of-the-art tools for semiconductor manufacturing, the semiconductor foundry has to ensure that there is maximum utilization of its tools and that this utilization also gives a good return on investments (RoI), thereby transforming high fixed costs into a competitive advantage for the market.

In addition, when a financial commitment is made by any financial institution or government, there should be a complete understanding of the overall goals, so as to be able to adjust the budget constraints under which neither credit is misused nor potential for success is starved of capital. This is very essential to keeping a steady flow and maximum utilization of capital for sustaining the progress of the capital-intensive semiconductor industry. Over half a century of progress of Moore's law has increased the power and decreased the costs of chips. Use of semiconductor chips to run a wide range of applications has resulted in an enormous economic growth by boosting productivity and increasing the consumers' purchasing power, in spite of no real increase in the actual wages. It has to be noted that high-tech semiconductor manufacturing being both knowledge-intensive and capital-intensive business, its progress has been associated with spending on R&D and organizational learning activities.

An Insight into the Semiconductor Manufacturing Process Driven by the Progress of Moore's Law

Since its inception in 1965 until recently, the 50 years of progress of Moore's law has been accompanied by the shrinking of the dimensions of transistors on an integrated circuit. The rapid advances in technology have enabled more components to be packaged onto a dense integrated circuit, thereby increasing the speed and lowering the costs of manufacture. In terms of this measurement, the commercial process technology has advanced from 10 μm in 1971 to 14 nm in 2014, which means that the microelectronic components that are fabricated on today's chips are roughly 700 times smaller than what they were three decades ago. While this progress of Moore's law in terms of boosting the productivity by shrinking the dimensions of transistors appears to be some simple idea, in reality, for the billions of microelectronic devices on the chip to work together, precise controls over a wide range of conditions of mass production are required.

These conditions include controlling processing temperatures, process timings, vibration levels, process pressure, and dust, almost everything is performed in a clean room. Any divergence from the optimal conditions could result in sharp increases in defect rates—they simply would not function properly. Establishing a control over these process conditions involves intensive trial and error, which cannot be carried out through the process design alone. As technology advances with the progress of Moore's law, newer process control parameters get introduced for every generation of technology. In fact, after the process technology of a newer generation has been designed, it takes considerable amount of time, up to a few years, for the fabrication plant to figure out how to control the defect rate, which could be as high as up to 95 percent initially, and it needs to be brought down to increase the RoI through mass production, else the process will not become commercially viable.

As technology advances with the progress of Moore's law, this newer technology also involves an increased amount of investments. A predictable RoI ensures more investments toward technological and economic growth. Besides, the size of silicon wafers has been steadily increasing over the years to ensure a better RoI. The cost of building a state-of-the-art semiconductor wafer fab today is approximately $10 billion and transition to 450-mm diameter silicon wafers is getting stalled due to poor RoI. Table 3.1 shows the rising costs of building wafer fabs from 1983 to 2007.

Table 3.1 The rising cost of building a leading-edge fab, 1983–2007

Year	1983	1990	1997	2001	2007
Wafer size (diameter in mm)	100	150	200	300	300
Line width (μm)	1.2	0.8	0.25	0.13	0.065
Cost (millions of USD)	200	400	1,250	3,000	5,000

Source: Adopted from Brown and Linden (2009, Table 2.1).

Transformation from Integrated Device Manufacturer to Fabless-Foundry Model

The semiconductor sector emerged in the United States emerged as an integral part of electronic devices manufacturing. As the semiconductor manufacturing technology was understood over a period of time, integrated device manufacturers (IDMs) demonstrated the advantage of spreading high fixed costs of capital-intensive semiconductor manufacturing over a high volume of customers by means of mass production of semiconductor wafers. This ability to mass produce enabled the IDM business model to prove to be very profitable. Hence, the predominant business model in global semiconductor industry at the advent of Moore's law was an IDM business model. Over the years several macroeconomic changes took place in the U.S. economy giving birth to new design houses. In order to ensure a full utilization by means of keeping the fabs in operation 24 × 7, IDMs started offering manufacturing services to independent design houses. This made it feasible for chip design to be separated from chip manufacturing.

Later in the 1980s, when Taiwan Semiconductor Manufacturing Corporation (TSMC) was started by Dr. Morris Chang, as a result of more collaboration, foundries were able to achieve much better economies of scale than IDMs due to their ability to cater to a broader range of customers. In addition, U.S. trade policies made it possible to have a much higher RoI for external shareholders of corporations by means of offshoring semiconductor manufacturing from the United States to Asian economies. Except for Intel (having deep pockets to invest) and Samsung (supported by the government of South Korea), most IDMs have offshored their manufacturing to Taiwan, Singapore, and China. This is how U.S. macroeconomic policies have played an important role in the transformation from IDM to fabless business model. In 2009, the microprocessor chip maker AMD was spun off and its foundry operation was separated from its design facility by establishing GlobalFoundries.

As a result of globalization policies, the foundry model has become a curse for those who were late to adopt it, because a much better established and mature manufacturing process used by reputable foundries like TSMC resulted in a much better yield than its competitors which has resulted in monopolization of market. However, by means of implementing proper macroeconomic policies, it is possible for every nation to have a viable semiconductor manufacturing ecosystem. It takes great vision and fortune to establish a state-of-the-art domestic semiconductor manufacturing industry and to keep it profitable. While the U.S. semiconductor manufacturing needs revival by means of back-shoring the jobs that were offshored from the United States, it is also useful to analyze the transformation of Chinese economy over years into one of the global manufacturing hubs for semiconductors. We will conclude this chapter with an understanding of what macroeconomic reforms would lead to a sustainable growth in China.

The Rise of China as an Industrial Powerhouse in Semiconductor Manufacturing

The rise of China as an industrial powerhouse needs to be analyzed in regard to its semiconductor manufacturing capabilities. This is because establishing a robust and high-quality semiconductor manufacturing ecosystem leads to growth of innovation and establishment of a knowledge-based economy. With the establishment of TSMC, Taiwan had started leveraging its huge investments in foundries to build a vibrant fabless sector. In spite of off-shoring assembly capabilities to Malaysia as early as 1970s; today Malaysia is still stuck in the low-end assembly segment and has not been able to drive the growth of its electronics industry beyond assembling of chips. Although India has leveraged its chip design capabilities and has high trade deficits from imported electronics due to its burgeoning middle class population, India has failed to establish a single profitable semiconductor fab until 2016. Hence, by learning the lesson about China's growth as a semi-conductor leader, several other developing economies could learn avoid making any mistakes made by China while establishing its semiconductor ecosystem, which have resulted in the crash of its stock markets in the summer of 2015. The following three core principles necessary for the success of any innovative enterprise, as suggested by Professor William Lazonick, have been taken into consideration when putting forth an innovative business model for driving the growth of global semiconductor industry:

- **Strategic success:** Majority of the decision-makers in an enterprise must have the willingness as well as capability to locate market entry points with long-term strategic implications. Semiconductor manufacturing is a long-term strategic investment and these investments pay off in the long run. Hence, the core decision-makers should be able to formulate a viable strategy to leverage existing technology, and make investments in physical and human capital with good timing. Timing of investments becomes critical as economy goes through its waxing and waning cycles. Hence, in an unbalanced economy, the timing to invest is best when the foundry has a huge demand for its products as it becomes fully operational. However, in case of a balanced economy, this timing does not become a bottleneck as there is plenty of economic demand to consume the supply of semiconductor wafers. Besides, there is no overproduction of wafers during an economic downturn.

- **Organizational success:** A top-notch semiconductor foundry should be able to attract, retain, train, and motivate its skilled workforce, particularly its seasoned technical and managerial staff, capable of adapting to constant technological migration. Hence, the foundry's management has to be sensitive to the needs of all employees. There has to be fairness in employee performance reviews and all employees have to be rewarded fairly in proportion to their throughput. This helps in employee retention contributing to organizational success, and experienced industry professionals are expected to outperform new college graduates because of their broad experience working in semiconductor industry.

- **Financial success**: In order to remain at the peak of technological development, any top-notch semiconductor wafer fab has to secure massive amount of long-term capital investment without undermining its strategic control.

There are several geopolitical risks involved in keeping the ownership of a foundry in the hands of any foreign investor, which could jeopardize the long-term sustainability as well as strategic control of the wafer fab.

The above three principles have been well endorsed in putting forth an innovative three-tier business model for the U.S. semiconductor industry based on the free market economic theory of *mass capitalism*. The proposed three-tier model is the only solution available for ensuring long-term sustainability and profitability in the U.S. semiconductor industry. Now, let us analyze the transformation of China's semiconductor industry over the years. Although Intel had its chip test and assembly sites in China since the 1990s, it established a foundry in China only in 2010. As mentioned previously, the timing for establishment of a top-notch foundry becomes critical in an unbalanced economy. Incorrect timing leads to cancellation of project and a huge loss of capital. Let us understand this with a practical example. In 1997, *Motorola* made an investment of around $1.9 billion to establish a state-of-the-art 200-mm megafab in Tianjin, China, with 0.25–0.35 μm process in order to produce around 20,000 wafers per month. However, semiconductor industry entered in a downturn in 1998 and hence *Motorola* delayed further investments until 2000.

When the fab was fully operational by 2001, there was a steep drop in international semiconductor prices. *Motorola* was out-competed by indigenous Chinese firms like Huawei and ZTE. Later it spun-off its semiconductor unit as *Freescale Semiconductors*, which showed no interest in owning costs of fabrication of chips in China. Prior to the spin-off, *Motorola* took a huge loss by selling off the Tianjin fab to Semiconductor Manufacturing International Corporation (SMIC) for $260 million. This shows the importance of timing when it comes to high-tech semiconductor manufacturing in an unbalanced economy. It also points to the importance of having a balanced economy for ensuring a robust economic demand and getting rid of the uncertainty about the timing of investment. When there is no uncertainty in the economy, more money will be invested into the economy driving the economic growth and increasing the economic solidarity. This way more job opportunities will be created and rising wages will increase consumer demand, thereby increasing the RoI.

China's National Policy After 2000 Leading to the Rise and Fall of the Chinese Dragon Economy

The rise of China as an industrial economic power has become an important topic of study. However, it has become equally important to understand how such a dominant economy crashed in the summer of 2015. Let us understand the industrial policies that have resulted in the rise and fall of the Chinese dragon economy. By studying this example, other developing countries could understand formulating correct policies leading to a long-term growth and profitability. Semiconductor manufacturing being a very capital-intensive and knowledge-intensive business, having a robust domestic semiconductor design and manufacturing industry leads to the progress of a knowledge-based economy. Hence, it is critical to understand where China went wrong. We will also study in this chapter the importance of the free market economic reforms that have to be undertaken by China in order to transition toward a robust and sustainable semiconductor manufacturing ecosystem.

The following are some of the key components of China's industrial policy for semiconductor as identified in Yin Li's research. In the early 2000s, China realized the importance of having foreign direct investments (FDI) into its economy in order to become a global manufacturing hub for semiconductors. With this ideology, there was a decisive shift in Chinese national policy and emergence of a less-hostile international trade regime, which resulted in changes in attitude toward doing business in China. In June 2000, the State Council issued a semiconductor policy document entitled, "Policies on Encouraging the Development of Software and Integrated Circuit Industry," which played an influential role in the rise of the Chinese domestic semiconductor industry. These policies have been a thoughtful departure from industrial policies of the 1990s, requiring government involvement in industry coordination and using domestic market to create national champions that could compete globally. The new industrial policy was based on promoting industrial development through deregulation, subsidies, tax incentives, FDI liberalization, investment in infrastructure, and science, education, and training programs as summarized below:

- **Tax break:** Five-year tax holiday starting from the first profit year for eligible semiconductor manufacturers making an investment exceeding 8 billion RMB and for a transistor line width smaller than 0.25micron. Another 50 percent cut in income tax rate for additional 5 years.
- **Value-added tax (VAT) exemption:** Seventeen percent VAT and import duty was exempted on imported raw materials and semiconductor manufacturing equipment and machinery. Any tariffs were to be eventually eliminated.
- **VAT rebates for domestically produced ICs:** Designers and producers can qualify for up to a 14 percent VAT rebate for domestically produced chips. By charging 17 percent VAT on imported semiconductors but only 3 percent for those produced domestically, China wanted to encourage domestic design and manufacture of products.
- **Infrastructure investment:** China allocated direct budgetary funds to local governments in order to provide a financial support for construction of infrastructure.
- **Foreign currency retention:** China increased its FOREX (FOreginEXchange) reserves by offering special accounts in the form of foreign currency for investors to put their after-tax profits if those profits would be used for future re-investment in China. Thereby, China ensured more investments into its economy rather than letting the profits from RoI investments repatriate back to their home countries.
- **Capital provision:** The state also provided assistance in the form of favored status and financial support to the establishment of venture capital firms. These firms were designed to play an important role in bringing up fabless semiconductor ecosystem in China.
- **National policy on treatment of foreigners:** The policies were applied to both foreign and domestically owned firms that qualify as per Article 52 of the semiconductor policy document.

- **Training programs:** Chinese universities were encouraged to offer courses and degrees on electronics engineering through increased budget allocations on the basis of increased enrollments.

Formulating the policies is one thing and implementing the same is a bigger challenge for any nation. As a WTO member, China had to become a signatory of the Information Technology Agreement (ITA), which required reducing tariffs on all ITA products, including semiconductors, to zero as of January 1, 2005. However, China played smart by manipulating the exchange rate of its currency in order to have a much better exchange rate with its trading partners. This helped trade in Chinese goods as they now appeared to be cheaper for the buyer. In this process, China also started running huge trade surplus with its trading partners resulting in a sharp increase in its FOREX reserves.

As a result of the above-mentioned policies, there was a huge and robust growth of nongovernment firms after the 2000s, leading to a growth of computer, telecommunications, and automobile industries. This is

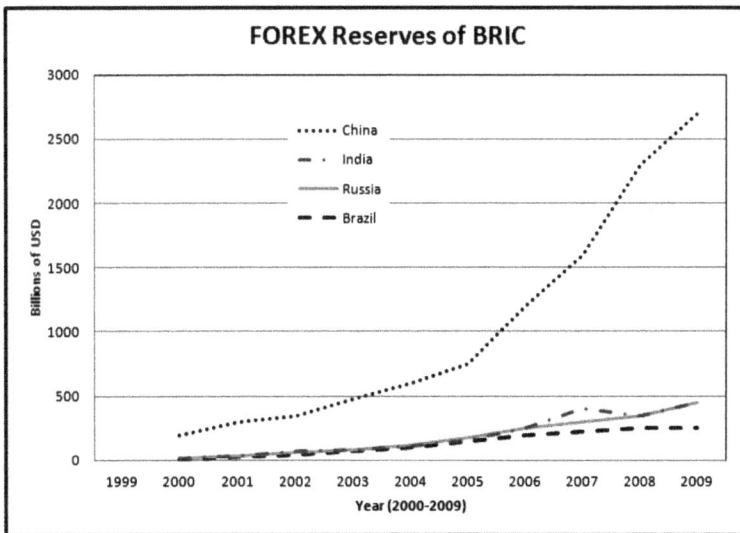

Figure 3.1 The growth in foreign exchange (FOREX) reserves of BRIC (Brazil, Russia, India, and China) after 2000

Source: Mass Capitalism: A Blueprint for Economic Revival (2014).

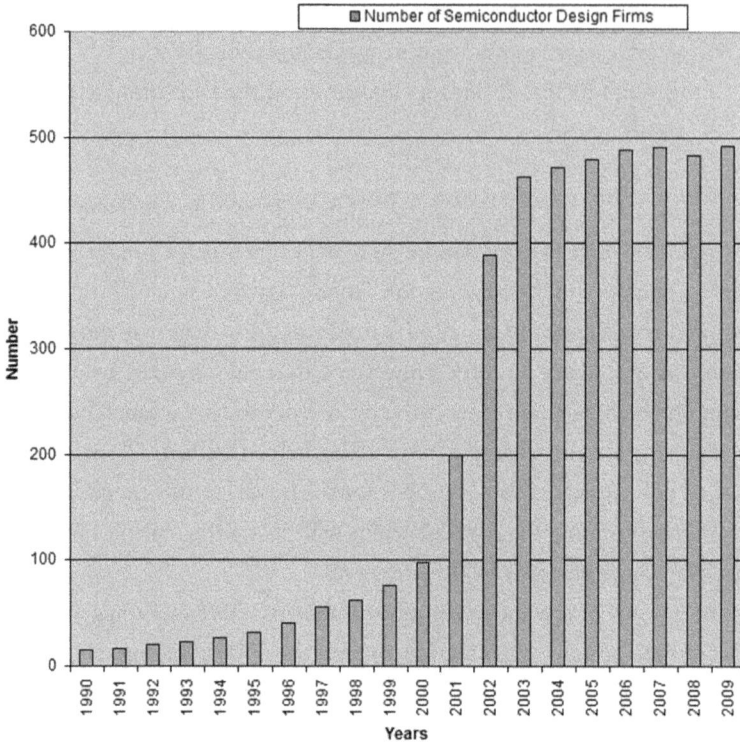

Figure 3.2 The growth of semiconductor design firms in China after 2000

Source: Reprinted from PWC, 2010, Figure 15.

obvious from the growth in the number of semiconductor design firms in China from 1999 to 2010.

U.S. exports control policy through the Semiconductor manufacturing Equipment and Materials (SEM) prevented China from developing advanced semiconductor manufacturing. Under the Wassenaar Arrangement, SEMs were classified as dual use technology (civilian and military use). Since the Cold War, the U.S. government was strict in adhering to these export controls. The General Accounting Office (GAO, 2002) estimated that the technology that was transferred to China was at least two generations older. However, transfer of any technology to any other nation hurts the transferring nation and this has become evident from the counterfeit electronics that China has been dumping into the U.S. Department of Defense Supply chain. I have elaborated this crisis further in Chapter

5, entitled "Mitigation of Counterfeit Electronics through US Macroeconomic Policies," in my volume *Mass Capitalism* (2014).

The big money ruling the democracy in the United States also played an important role in helping the transfer of high-tech semiconductor manufacturing technology to China. In 2002, a report on SEM export controls to China by the U.S. GAO first challenged the effectiveness of the existing export control methods that were formulated during the Cold War mainly due to the foreign availability of comparable technologies (GAO, 2002). Since then, the U.S. export control was increasingly shifting the focus onto the recipients, rather than the items involved in export. As a result, in 2003, SMIC, the world's third largest capital spender on SEM in that year, obtained a special import/export license from the U.S. government allowing it to import the most advanced fab tools from the United States. In 2007, under a new program of the U.S. Department of Commerce called the Validated End-User program, three semiconductor firms in China were certificated as "trusted" end-users to import controlled items, including Applied Materials China Ltd., SMIC, and HHNEC (GAO, 2008, p. 17). U.S. SEM suppliers applauded the policy change, arguing that the new program will "make U.S. exports more competitive in China" (Leopold, 2007). Indeed, by 2006, China's spending on semiconductor equipment, mainly imported from abroad, had already reached $1.6 billion (GAO, 2008). However, the U.S. policy-makers failed to take note of the fact that China has been steadily dumping counterfeit electronics into the U.S. supply chains and with manufacturing plants disappearing from the United States and moving to China, this has now become a national security threat for the United States.

China also played smart by not competing directly with the foreign chipmakers as its industry developed, but instead, the Chinese foundry positioned as contract manufacturer for both domestic and foreign chip designers. This strategy was possible only because of extensive business contacts of the expatriate techno-entrepreneurs who had repatriated back to China due to government and industrial policies of China. Such a contract manufacturing business model expanded the customer base of the foundry and released the customer base from the limits of the Chinese market. It increased revenue, and enabled the advanced production lines to be utilized in better ways through manufacturing state-of-the-art chips for leading fabless companies. In addition to its sound industrial policies, the semiconductor industry in China also adopted a Western style of management.

Since 2000s, there was a drive to attract several Western-educated Chinese individuals to help contribute to the growth of Chinese semiconductor ecosystem by offering them generous stock options and other benefits. The Chinese government tried to follow a style of governance, which included strategy, organization, as well as finance of nongovernment semiconductor companies to that of Western business strategies and structures, in order to usher in innovation. Since the semiconductor business enterprises were founded and managed by expatriate techno-entrepreneurs, they had the most capable decision makers who were available in China. However, just like the Western business enterprises, a major concern for exercise of strategic control in these nongovernment Chinese enterprises was the fact that the authority of techno-managers was undermined by providers of capital. This is precisely what resulted in the growing wage–productivity gap not just in the Chinese semiconductor industry but in its overall economy.

A rising gap between wages and productivity creates an oversupply and poor domestic demand. This results from the external shareholders dominating the corporate board of directors resulting in this wage–productivity gap to grow further. Let us take an example of SMIC to understand this problem. After its Initial Public Offering (IPO), the shares of SMIC were distributed to a variety of foreign and Chinese entities. The internal SMIC management team held as little as a 28 percent share of the company, allowing managerial control to be separated from the share ownership. In order to serve their political ends, the Chinese State-Owned Enterprises (SOEs) started owning more shares of SMIC. As a result of SOE being the majority shareholder, there was a major change in SMIC's board of directors. After its IPO, in 2004 SMIC had only two directors out of eight with a close connection to organizations linked to the Chinese state, Shanghai Industrial Holdings (Shanghai government) and Beida Jade. However, in 2010, three directors out of six came from Chinese SOEs with two of them appointed by Datang Telecom and one by Shanghai Industrial Holdings.

This is precisely what has led to an increased bureaucracy and less focus on innovation but more focus of the company to please the politicians.

Thus, It has resulted in government intervention into the Chinese economy. Too much government intervention into the economy cripples entrepreneurship and innovation and instead of talented employees getting a fair share for their hard work and innovations, their share of profits goes into the hands of external shareholders. Unlike the United States where the external shareholders in semiconductor industry are the private financial investors, China had external shareholders in the form of Chinese SOEs. As the dominance of external shareholders grows, it results in stock market speculations and loss of overall economic balance. In this way, when employees are not the majority shareholders in a big enterprise, the wage–productivity gap grows too big, eventually resulting in crash of corporate profits and hence crash of stock markets as there is no sufficient demand to cater to the rising supply of goods. This growing gap between wages and productivity is precisely what has led to a crash of China's stock markets in the summer of 2015. This crash of China's stock market has sent shockwaves across the world and has also resulted in a rising wave against policies of globalization in most developed economies. China is also facing backlash from many countries in its latest global spending spree and hence China should invest its capital on domestic economic growth by pursuing free market economic reforms based on *mass capitalism* rather than go on a global spending spree.

Conclusion

The growth of Chinese semiconductor industry resulting from the offshoring of manufacturing operations from U.S. fabless semiconductor industry after 2000 has resulted in the transformation of Chinese economy from a government-controlled enterprise to a nongovernment enterprise for semiconductor industry. It was in order to lower the manufacturing costs because of the incentives that were offered by Chinese government that had attracted U.S.-based MNCs to offshore their manufacturing to China. This offshoring of manufacturing to Asia has resulted in the transformation of major part of the U.S. semiconductor industry from IDM to a fabless-foundry business model. Although it resulted in macroeconomic losses to the U.S. economy, it has resulted in the transformation of Chinese economy as a global manufacturing hub of electronics. It was the relentless progress of Moore's law based on supply-side economic policies and a desire to achieve high profitability for external shareholders of corporations in the U.S. semiconductor industry, which resulted in the offshoring of manufacturing operations to China.

However, due to the external ownership of majority shares of Chinese foundries post IPO, the resulting economic system could not stop the gap between wages and productivity from growing beyond any acceptable standards. This growing gap between wages and productivity eventually caused a crash of China's stock markets in the summer of 2015. Since its economic crash, China has been pursuing economic reforms to transform its economy from an export-oriented economy to a sustainable domestic economy in order to avoid any more economic troubles as a result of the problems happening in global economy. However, as Chinese government and businesses undertake these economic reforms, they have to be aware of the fact that China's economy crashed because of the growing gap between wages and productivity.

Additionally, since advanced semiconductor manufacturing industry requires significant capital investments, the support from local government is critical to keep the industry sustainable. However, in order to have a free market economy, the intervention of the government into the economy should be minimal. As Chinese foundries were unable to stop intervention of Chinese SOEs in controlling the board of directors and hence the corporate management's policies of these foundries, China could not control the gap between wages and productivity from growing beyond acceptable means. This is why state capitalism of China has proven to be a failure just like crony capitalism in the United States. Therefore, China needs to undertake free market economic reforms in order to achieve sustainability and profitability of its semiconductor industry.

China can achieve true free markets in its semiconductor industry by undertaking economic reforms based on the theory of *mass capitalism*, which would ensure that wages would catch up with productivity thereby ensuring that economic demand catches up with the supply of goods produced in the economy. A three-tier business model for semiconductor industry would help make this industry both sustainable and profitable in the long run. It would transform the Chinese economy and put it at the forefront of technological development. An absence of economic reforms based on *mass capitalism* would result in an imbalanced economic growth leading to a poor utilization of available resources. *Mass capitalism* will prove to be a blueprint for the transformation of Chinese semiconductor industry into an economic and financial powerhouse, which would prove to be a role model to be emulated by other developing countries such as India, which are struggling to have their own indigenous semiconductor manufacturing industry in order to control their ever-growing trade deficits resulting from import of electronic goods.

Suggested Readings

[1] Li, Yin, *From Classic Failures to Global Competitors: Business Organization and Economic Development in the Chinese Semiconductor Industry*, University of Massachusetts Lowell, Lowell, MA, 2011.

[2] Mulay, Apek, *Mass Capitalism: A Blueprint for Economic Revival*, Book Publishers Network, Bothell, WA, 2014.

[3] Mulay, Apek, *Sustaining Moore's Law: Uncertainty Leading to a Certainty of IoT Revolution*, Morgan & Claypool Publishers, San Rafael, CA, 2015.

CHAPTER 4

International Technology Roadmap for Semiconductors

Its Past, Present, and Future

Introduction

There are several steps involved in the manufacture of integrated circuits (ICs) or any semiconductor product which include the process steps such as photolithography, etching, metal deposition, etc. As the semiconductor industry evolved, each of these operations was typically performed by specialized machines built by a variety of commercial companies. If there is progress of only one semiconductor manufacturing step but no progress of others then it becomes difficult for the industry to advance, since in many cases it does no good for a company to introduce a new product if the other necessary steps are not available around the same time. By means of having a technology roadmap, there would be a well-defined goal that would give an idea as to when a certain capability will be needed. This makes the business model more predictable by letting each supplier target a specific date to complete their piece of the puzzle.

The fabless business model has democratized innovation over the years with a progressive externalization of production tools to the suppliers of specialized equipment. Hence, a need arose for a clear roadmap in order to anticipate the evolution of the market and to plan and control the technological needs of IC production. For several years, the Semiconductor

Industry Association (SIA) gave this responsibility of coordination to the United States, which led to the creation of an American-style roadmap, the National Technology Roadmap for Semiconductors (NTRS).

In 1998, the SIA became closer to its European, Japanese, Korean, and Taiwanese counterparts by creating the first global roadmap: the International Technology Roadmap for Semiconductors (ITRS). This international group includes (as of the 2003 edition) 936 companies that were affiliated with working groups within the ITRS. The organization was divided into 17 Technical Working Groups (TWGs), with each TWG focusing on a key element of the technology and associated supply chain. Traditionally, the ITRS roadmap was updated in even years, and completely revised in odd years.

Paolo Gargini's Analysis of the Past, Present, and Future of ITRS

ITRS chairperson Paolo Gargini, in a presentation entitled "ITRS: Past, Present and Future" published in February 2015, has laid out a roadmap for the global semiconductor industry for years to come. The ITRS Chair, an IEEE fellow, takes us on a journey of the progress of semiconductor industry from 1959 until recent years, where the industry has been driven by the progress of Moore's law.

In 1965, Intel cofounder Gordon Moore, in "Cramming More Components onto Integrated Circuits" in *Electronics Magazine* (April 19, 1965), made the observation that, in the history of computing hardware, the number of transistors on ICs doubles approximately every 2 years. This law is now used in the semiconductor industry to guide long-term planning and to set targets for research and development.

The capabilities (processing speed, memory capacity, sensors) of many digital electronic devices have been improving at roughly exponential rates and are, thereby, strongly linked to Moore's law. This exponential technological improvement in the electronic devices has dramatically enhanced the impact of digital electronics in nearly every segment of today's world economy. Indeed, Moore's law has been behind the technological advancements and socioeconomic developments in the late 20th and early 21st centuries.

From International Electron Device Meeting (IEDM) held in December 1975 to Micro Tech 2000 Workshop held in 1991, Moore's law has been the driver behind the R&D initiatives of the SIA. The most significant trend in the progress of Moore's law has been the decreasing cost-per-function, which has led to significant improvements in economic productivity and the overall quality of life through proliferation of computers, communication, and other industrial and consumer electronics. It was SIA that initiated the NTRS in 1992 with the basic premise that the continued scaling of electronics would further reduce the cost per function and promote market growth for ICs.

As time progressed, SIA was joined by corresponding industry associations in Europe, Japan, South Korea, and Taiwan to participate in a 1998 update of the roadmap and to begin work toward the first ITRS, published in 1999. The overall objective of the ITRS is to present industry wide consensus on the "best current estimate" of the industry's R&D needs out to a 15-year horizon. Now, there are more developing economies, such as India and China, that are about to join the ITRS to drive the progress of Moore's law; these countries also want to have a larger viable domestic semiconductor industry that provides good paying jobs in their respective economies. In this way, the ITRS has provided a platform to improve the quality of R&D investment decisions made at all levels and has thus helped channel research efforts to areas that most need research breakthroughs.

The 2010 update to the ITRS had growth slowing at the end of 2013, after which transistor counts and densities are to double only every 3 years. Accordingly, since 2007 the ITRS had addressed the concept of functional diversification under the title "More-than-Moore." This concept addressed as an emerging category of devices that incorporate functionalities that do not necessarily scale according to Moore's law, but provide additional value to the end customer in different ways. The *More-than-Moore* approach includes the non-digital functionalities (e.g., RF communication, power control, passive components, sensors, actuators) to migrate from the system board-level into a particular package-level (i.e., SiP) or chip-level (i.e., SoC) system solution. ITRS also hopes that by 2020, it will be possible to augment the technology of constructing integrated circuits (CMOS) by introducing new devices that will realize some "beyond CMOS" capabilities. SoC and SiP technologies are expected to provide a path for continued improvement in performance, power, cost, and size at the system level without relying upon conventional CMOS scaling alone. The SiP technology is rapidly evolving from specialty technology used in a narrow set of applications to a high-volume technology with wide-ranging impact on electronics markets.

Moore's law has had an amazing run for the past several decades with an unmeasured economic impact on the U.S. semiconductor industry. The progress of Moore's law has even transformed the business model of the U.S. semiconductor industry and continues to do so. It is an open secret that, for a variety of reasons, the U.S. manufacturing base has sharply deteriorated over the past three decades, and the U.S. semiconductor industry is no exception to this trend. In fact, this industry may have suffered harder than some other American enterprises. Other nations imported technology from gullible American companies, and, with their low real wages, out-competed U.S. firms all over the world. The rest is history. By now many American industries have disappeared, while most others have shrunk, resulting in a loss of jobs and stagnant wages. When the great recession struck in 2007, the lingering weakness of the American economy, so far ignored by experts and the government, came to the surface.

Now the immense problems such as lack of skilled workforce, youth unemployment, huge capital investments, unsustainable trade and budget deficits, as well as manufacturing complexities are contributing to a bankruptcy of economic wisdom and are making it difficult to sustain Moore's law and maintain its economic impact on the semiconductor industry. There is, hence, an urgent need for new ideas to deal constructively with these business and economic issues affecting the very survival of the semiconductor industry and the resulting knowledge-based economy. With this in mind, ITRS has incorporated *More-than-Moore* and Radio Frequency (RF)/Analog Mixed Signal (AMS) chapters in the main body of the ITRS. While ITRS is uncertain as to whether this would be sufficient to encompass the plethora of associated technologies now entangled into modern products, ITRS believes that the multifaceted public consumer has become an influential driver of the semiconductor industry through an ever-increasing demand of custom functionality in commercial electronic products. In other words, the ITRS has finally realized that the forces driving the supply of silicon for progressing Moore's law can only be sustained as long as there is an economic demand for them. However, in my research I have discovered that ITRS has not yet proposed any economic solution for the semiconductor industry in order to boost the consumer demand for semiconductor products.

The following are the conclusions that ITRS arrived at in their February 2015 meeting:

1. It was the "geometrical scaling" that led the semiconductor industry for three decades.
2. A cooperative and distributive research and manufacturing methodology is a cost-effective means of reducing cost.
3. Organizations like Focus Center Research Program (FCRP), National Research Institute (NRI), Semiconductor Manufacturing Technology (SEMATECH), International Medical Equipment Collaborative (IMEC), and other government organizations have actively cooperated in advanced research.
4. It was an "equivalent scaling" that saved the semiconductor industry since the beginning of the previous decade and International Technical Working Group (ITWG) has brought new ideas through an international collaboration.
5. The shipments of cell phones and tablets surpassed PCs in 2010, showing a growing trend toward handheld and portable electronics as compared to PCs.
6. New architectures have been proposed in post-CMOS devices to drive the progress of Moore's law such as 3D scaling, FinFET scaling, nanowire/tunnel FET, etc.
7. The incubation time for any new technological driver is approximately 12–15 years.

Critiquing the Macroeconomics of the ITRS *More-than-Moore* and *Beyond-CMOS* Approach

The electronics industry has been mourning the potential demise of Moore's law for a long time. I think it is too soon to start planning the funeral. In an article by Richard Gray, entitled "Are the Chips Down for

Moore's Law? Computer Industry Admits It Is struggling to Keep up with the Pace of Innovation," published on February 11, 2016 in DailyMail. com, the author makes the following claim:

> The semiconductor industry, which has used the observation made by Intel co-founder Gordon Moore as its target development in recent decades, is now set to abandon the approach. The move is thought to be a reflection that companies are struggling to keep up with the pace of innovation required to cram ever more transistors onto a finite space.

As a Moore's law enthusiast and author of two other volumes about the semiconductor industry before authoring this present volume, I must vehemently object because I believe that Moore's law has a bright future. I am not referring solely to the immediate future, but also to the ways that this approach could benefit greatly from the fourth industrial revolution in the form of the *IoT*.

According to the ITRS, the industry body that sets out the direction that industry would adopt, it had held its final meeting in Atlanta, Georgia, around mid-February 2016 in order to lay out its plans for semiconductor industry roadmap for up to year 2030. While I am certainly glad that the focus of ITRS meeting was to define new drivers for the industry as a way to create a path of productivity and profitability, the ITRS plans to follow *"More-than-Moore"* and *"Beyond-CMOS"* approach that will take into consideration a top-down system-driven roadmap framework but will not take into consideration the real macroeconomic policy related reasons because of which the economics of semiconductor manufacturing is leading to a demise of Moore's law.

I might be the only semiconductor industry analyst who is not just optimistic about the future of Moore's law but who has also provided a concrete solution to sustain the productivity and profitability resulting from the progress of Moore's law. In order to sustain profitability of any project, a proper macroeconomic policy is essential because the RoI on any project depends on the health of macroeconomy, which is nothing but the basic forces of supply and demand.

The industry analysts who are today pessimistic as well as those who have been pessimistic in the past about the progress of Moore's law have not studied or understood the macroeconomics behind forecasted demise of Moore's law. As quoted from my second volume *Sustaining Moore's Law* (2015),

> While Moore's Law progressed predictably on the physical side as transistor dimensions shrank, macroeconomics was completely ignored by the American businesses. Over the past 50 years, Moore's Law has been scaling at all costs and ignoring macro-economy. Moore's Law can easily continue for the foreseeable future if the chip manufacturing industry becomes sustainable by having a balanced economy. That will require some major macro-economic reforms for eliminating the gap between supply and demand caused by the gap between wages and productivity. Restoring a free-market economy in the U.S. will not only ensure the progress of high technology and innovation, thereby sustaining the progress of Moore's Law, but will also help the global semi-conductor industry progress to 450 mm diameter silicon wafers in order to improve its profitability from mass production.

When ITRS takes into consideration a top-down system-driven approach, I would highly recommend that they implement policies for ensuring a sustainable macroeconomic progress that goes beyond reforming the existing business models, supply chains, and corporate board of management structure. The initial focus shall be on reviving the industry- and knowledge-based global economy with simple yet practical solutions. The second phase would usher in a fourth industrial revolution in the form of IoT while learning from the mistakes of the third industrial revolution, which violated parameters of macroeconomics leading to an unsustainable growth and an early demise of Moore's law.

In the following chapters, I have explained to a greater detail my proposed approach of minimum necessities and maximum amenities that would sustain the consumer demand for advanced electronic gadgets, which would in turn increase investments in global semiconductor industry and further the circulation of currency within an economy. Additionally, a

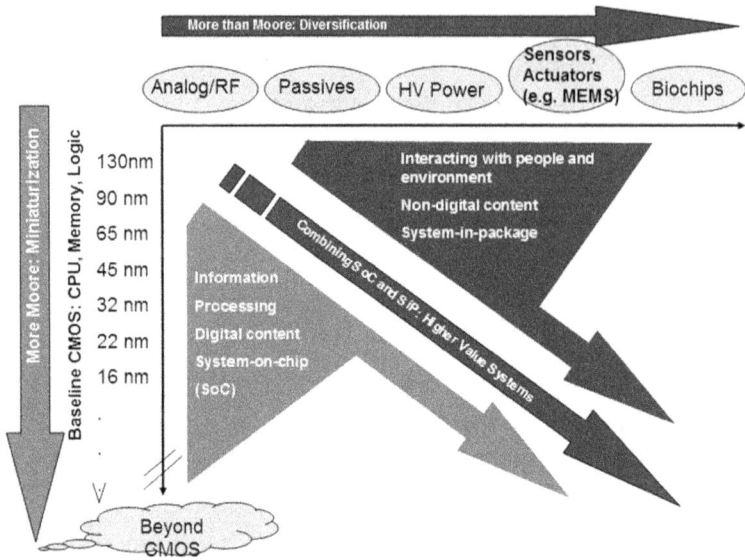

Figure 4.1 Driver for More-than-Moore and Beyond CMOS

Source: 2011 ITRS Executive Summary Fig. 4.

transition to 450-mm silicon wafers has the potential to not only help the manufacturers in the industry but it would also help the end consumers. This transition to 450-mm diameter silicon wafers is critical to address the ongoing problem of an economic stagnation in the global economy.

In their February 2015 meeting, the business model proposed by ITRS for 2020 and beyond appears to be very similar to the Integrated Device Manufacturer (IDM) Business Model of the 1970s. Either it is a virtual IDM model or I believe that this proposal aims to be based on being able to have sufficient capital and deeper collaboration between different drivers of *More-than-Moore* and *Beyond CMOS* when it comes to system integration. There are several new drivers put forth by ITRS for 2020 and beyond as shown in Figure 4.1.

In addition to the above drivers, ITRS has also provided an assessment of various driving forces for *More-than-Moore* and *Beyond CMOS* while ushering in the fourth industrial revolution in the form of IoT, as shown in Figure 4.2.

In the subsequent chapters of this volume, we will discuss where the semiconductor industry stands as of today and whether anything has been

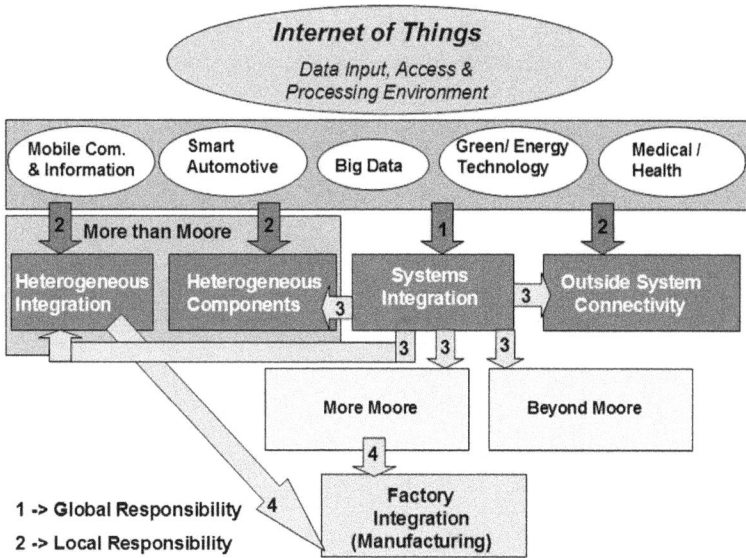

Figure 4.2 An assessment of driving forces for Industry 4.0 through more-than-Moore and Beyond CMOS drivers

Source: ITRS, Feb 2015.

missed in the analysis of ITRS. Additionally, we will also look into how to envision these ideas for *More-than-Moore* and *Beyond CMOS* while providing a roadmap for the progress of the semiconductor industry. The contribution of Moore's observation to global GDP growth has been approximately 20 percent. The semiconductor industry and ITRS have an opportunity to play a major role in sustaining this growth by means of implementing smart macroeconomic policies.

Suggested Readings

[1] Wikipedia, '*International Technology Roadmap for Semiconductors*'. https://en.wikipedia.org/wiki/International_Technology_Roadmap_for _Semiconductors

[2] Gargini, Paolo, '*ITRS - Past, Present and Future*'. February 2015.

[3] Mulay, Apek, *Mass Capitalism: A Blueprint for Economic Revival*, Book Publishers Network, Bothell, WA, 2014.

[4] Mulay, Apek, *Sustaining Moore's Law: Uncertainty Leading to a Certainty of IoT Revolution*, Morgan & Claypool Publishers, San Rafael, CA, 2015.

CHAPTER 5

Fabless versus Integrated Device Manufacturer

Introduction

The technology boom years of the 1970s were associated with the Integrated Device Manufacturer (IDM) business model, when all top manufacturers of semiconductors maintained a vertically integrated business model: designing, testing, and building their products. Then, in the early 1980s, small manufacturers began entering the marketplace. Due to huge capital investments, there were huge barriers to the entry. Hence, IDMs were producing more chips than they could actually use in their products. As this surplus continued to grow due to rapid growth of semiconductor industry, it led to the creation of a fabless business model. The term "fabless" means that the company does not manufacture the silicon wafers, or chips, used in its products; instead, it outsources the work to a manufacturing plant, or foundry. In this chapter, we compare these two business models and their relative advantages and disadvantages from a macroeconomic perspective.

A Brief History of Integrated Device Manufacturer and Fabless Business Model

A semiconductor company that designs, manufactures, and tests in-house can be considered as an IDM. Historically, it was the semiconductor sector of the electronics industry in which a vertical specialization took place. As specialized merchant producers, IDMs such as *Texas Instruments, National Semiconductors, and Fairchild Semiconductors* were established during the 1960s. The success of IDM business model led to a further vertical integration in the electronics industry. However, the continued technological progress driven by the progress of Moore's law has resulted in much greater costs of manufacturing for future technology nodes.

In addition to the above, the IDM business model also created a huge barrier for new designs from small design firms to enter into the semiconductor market place. This is because of the huge barriers of significantly large capital investments for making an entry into the semiconductor manufacturing sector. This resulted in the birth of the fabless-foundry business model in the 1980s. The fabless semiconductor companies specialize only in development and marketing of new innovative designs. They outsource the actual manufacturing of their silicon wafers. This development has spurred the creation of a new generation of contract semiconductor wafer manufacturers called "foundries."

It was with a heavy assistance from the Taiwanese government that the Taiwan Semiconductor Manufacturing Corporation (TSMC) and United Microelectronics Corporation (UMC) were established in the 1980s as independent semiconductor foundries. These two became industry leaders as "pure-play semiconductor foundry." This resulted in the entry of new design firms, which had to focus on innovative designs without having to worry about the huge manufacturing costs for running a state-of-the-art semiconductor foundry, also called a "Fab." It led to a new era of phenomenal growth of fabless businesses. New successful fabless semiconductor companies like Qualcomm, Broadcom, NVIDIA, etc., ushered in a new era of growth of the global semiconductor industry.

Impact of Globalization of Semiconductor Manufacturing on Fabless and IDM Business Models

Globalization of semiconductor manufacturing has resulted in offshoring of high-paying manufacturing jobs from the United States to countries like Japan in the past and now to China. Although this practice has resulted in huge microeconomic profits for companies based in the United States, it has caused considerable macroeconomic losses for the U.S. economy. With the offshoring of high-paying jobs, Americans have to depend on relatively low-paying service sector jobs. In addition to that, this process has also resulted in transfer of technology and innovation from the United States to Asian economies over the years.

The "trade deficits" for the United States resulting from the absence of true free trade between the United States and Asian economies have resulted in a loss of FOReignEXchange (FOREX) reserves for the United States and also caused an exponential growth of FOREX reserves for the Asian economies, thereby transferring economic and financial power to the hands of Japan and China, alongwith manufacturing technology and innovation. In addition, low wages of Americans have diminished their consumer purchasing power so much that they have become accustomed to buying cheap goods from China coming into the U.S. markets. The resulting trade deficits from such practices have made it impossible for the United States to revive its economy, and poverty in the United States today is the highest of the last 50 years.

The concept behind the evolution of the fabless semiconductor industry was outsourcing the capital-intensive manufacturing operations and focusing on innovative circuit designs. The fabless semiconductor companies in the United States have preferred to make use of TSMC as their foundry since 1987. Hence, the fabless semiconductor business model has over the years contributed greatly to U.S. trade deficits. Today, *GlobalFoundries* could play a big role in reducing and eliminating U.S. trade deficits by manufacturing semiconductor wafers for fabless semiconductor companies in the United States with its Fab 8 foundry in Malta, New York. Another drawback of the globalization of semiconductor manufacturing is the entry of counterfeit electronics into the U.S. defense supply chain. As per the General Accounting Office (GAO), nearly 40 percent of U.S. Department of Defense (DoD) supply chain is filled with defective or counterfeit goods, thereby threatening U.S. national security. The economic causes for the same have been elaborated in-depth in Chapter 5, entitled "Mitigation of Counterfeit Electronics through US Macroeconomic Policies," of my first volume, *Mass Capitalism* (2014).

As U.S. corporate policies of globalization have resulted in lower manufacturing costs owing to manufacturing from Asian fabs, and importing of those cheaply manufactured goods back into the United States without any import duty, because of free trade, it has resulted in an exponential growth of fabless semiconductor industry that used Asian fabs to manufacture their chips. As a result of higher profits to shareholders provided by fabless semiconductor industries, the nonemployee external shareholders of many IDMs have also forced these IDMs to offshore their manufacturing operations to Asian economies. In this way, several IDMs based in the United States have spun-off their manufacturing business and become fabless. Thereby, globalization of semiconductor manufacturing has played a key role in the transformation of U.S. semiconductor industry. However, credit goes to the mutual collaboration that exists between the fabless semiconductor companies and their foundry partners. This cooperative collaboration has been one of the reasons of the success of the fabless semiconductor industry.

The Concept of Virtual IDM for the Semiconductor Industry

In his keynote speech at ConFab 2012 in Las Vegas, Nevada, entitled "The Next Transformation of the Semiconductor Industry," *John Chen*, PhD, VP of technology and foundry operations at NVIDIA Corporation, coined the term virtual IDM. As per John, the virtual IDM is a way for semiconductor foundries, fabless companies, and outsource semiconductor assembly and test (OSAT) houses to collaborate in order to solve the new challenges in technology, manufacturing, and business. The challenges in technology are huge, and while the IDM business model has preserved manufacturing jobs within the United States, fabless semiconductor companies have eventually created more small businesses and hence more innovations in the semiconductor industry. However, as a result of offshored manufacturing, the fabless business model has resulted in huge and unsustainable trade deficits as well as budget deficits. Hence, for the virtual IDM concept to become truly successful, the advantages achieved from fabless semiconductor business model, which leads to a cooperative collaboration between the businesses and creates more small businesses, need to be preserved; the drawbacks of fabless business model, which lead to trade and budget deficits, need to be eliminated. That way the virtual IDM concept can in usher the next transformation of the semiconductor industry.

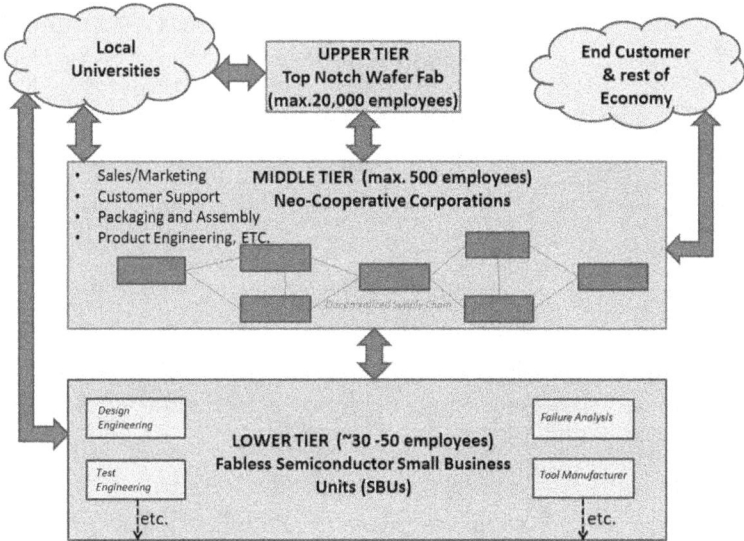

Figure 5.1 A three-tier business model for the global semiconductor industry. The upper tier is a top-notch wafer fab, and fabless small businesses comprise the lower tier. The middle, and most important, tier has neo-cooperative corporations, which have exchange relationships as a decentralized supply chain. The middle industrial tier connects the other two industrial tiers with the rest of the economy

Source: Mass Capitalism: A Blueprint for Economic Revival (2014).

Hence, I propose a three-tier fabless-foundry business model for global semiconductor industry based on the free market economic theory of *mass capitalism* that would usher in this virtual IDM model and make it sustainable with free market balanced economic policies. A balanced economy is critical for the semiconductor industry to reach its next level of innovation and financial success. An economy is balanced when it does not have any trade and budget deficits, which keep supply and demand in balance. Such a balanced economy would increase domestic consumer purchasing power by letting the wages of workers catch up with their productivity. Further, to prevent foreign countries from taking control of the economy by accumulating huge FOREX reserves, macroeconomic reforms are critical to move away from the temptation of globalization and ensure sustainable local productivity and economy, which would eliminate trade deficits.

Upper Tier—Semiconductor Manufacturing from a Top-notch Wafer Fab

A top-notch wafer fab needs an investment larger than what is needed for a nuclear reactor. In 2013, the cost of building the next-generation wafer fab was estimated at over $10 billion. The location of a wafer fab depends upon the ready availability of all necessary raw materials needed for manufacturing. The local government should build the necessary infrastructure, like a domestic or international airport, good transportation facilities, good infrastructure, etc., for a smooth delivery of the goods to end customers. This would ensure the growth of smaller and medium-size businesses that would cater to that fab. Any infrastructure investment would be a long-term investment to attract other businesses.

In order to have a balanced economy, the official monetary policy should be such that wages keep up with labor productivity. Since workers' wages contribute to consumer demand and workers' productivity contributes to the supply of goods, when wages catch up with productivity, supply and demand grow and fall together. Hence, it is important that company profits are first shared among the employees in proportion to their productive contributions and then later with outside investors. In order to ensure that wages catch up with productivity, there should be special incentives—a share of the profits—offered to highly productive and innovative employees. The remaining profits, if any, should be shared with the private investors as return on their investments. It is very important for an economy first to ensure that wages catch up with productivity to maintain a rational distribution of wages. This would also eliminate any economic imbalance that might result from huge wage disparities.

While company profits should be shared across the board in proportion to productive contributions of employees, these fabs, although government backed, should have complete autonomy to lay off lazy and unproductive employees. This model would ensure that the wafer fab remains a top-notch fab and at the forefront of innovation. Additionally, it would rectify the inefficiencies that may have existed in government-sponsored businesses. Similarly, by letting the employees' wages to catch up with their productivity, it would ensure high consumer purchasing power in the economy.

For the semiconductor industry to be financially successful, it is critical that money circulates in the economy and does not remain idle in bank vaults or other forms of valueless hoardings. To make this feasible, it would be best for a wafer fab to offer retirement schemes to its employees such that employees can invest some of their income toward the growth of their company by purchasing company shares. In this manner, a wafer fab can raise much-needed additional capital from its own employees, while its employees become part-owners.

This model has two benefits. Since employees own some shares of the wafer fab, they will work hard toward the success of the foundry. In economic downturns, these wafer fabs would prefer to share losses by taking across-the-board wage cuts or by cutting work hours of workers rather than laying them off. This would essentially maintain balance in the supply of goods and their demand. Additionally, since massive job losses due to layoffs could be minimized in economic downturns, it would also minimize government spending and hence budget deficits for offering unemployment benefits for laid-off workers.

In order to engender accountability and transparency in employees' performance reviews, individual departments inside wafer fabs should be decentralized so that different engineering teams are grouped into smaller teams that elect their respective representatives onto the corporate management board in a democratic way. This would enable employees to voice their concerns to the management through their representatives. These employee representatives on the management board would work with other members of the management board to ensure their decisions, supported by the majority, are in the best interest of employees and hence of the company, thereby engendering a healthy relationship between the employees and management.

A good wafer fab should also collaborate with local universities by offering cooperative internships to engineering students and technicians. This model would enable a foundry to offer challenging thesis projects to students pursuing masters in engineering through cooperative internships. The wafer fab should also offer doctoral research fellowships or assistantships so that these doctoral students would essentially work for the company at a fraction of the salary of regular research employees; this is the most economical way to fund R&D.

- Doctoral students' research can be sponsored by this university–companies conglomerate, and then the resulting technologies (developed by the doctoral students) are spun off into new companies, which are owned partly by this conglomerate and partly by the doctoral students and their supervisors. They would become future entrepreneurs of the semiconductor industry and be a part of the lower tier of this business model. Such conglomerates open up equal opportunity for material and intellectual advancement to all students.
- The doctoral student-owners are then free to employ their master's degree graduates in their companies and implement a system of employee profit-sharing. This would also help students to receive a financial aid and help the semiconductor foundry get its R&D work done at much lower costs from the doctoral and Master's students.

Lower Tier—The Fabless Semiconductor Businesses

An established top-notch wafer fab would also create local businesses, which provide necessary tools, test equipment, engineering services, etc., for a smooth functioning of the wafer fab. These providers of different services, in addition to the fabless semiconductor businesses, would form the lower tier of this three-tier business model. In order to ensure sufficient job creation in the local economy, the fabless industry should undergo decentralization when it comes to offering these engineering services. Small business units (SBUs) should offer engineering services, such as circuit design engineering, circuit layout engineering, test development engineering, failure analysis, tool manufacturing and maintenance, etc.

Each engineering service provider should work as an independent SBU with a maximum of 30 to 50 employees in each business unit. These SBUs should comply with local antitrust laws, which should be strictly enforced by local government to avoid any mergers and acquisitions (M&As), which lead to job losses when M&As occur between companies with similar portfolios. Some of the existing fabless corporations are too big, and they use their huge profits to acquire small businesses. These mergers restrict competition, which has resulted in monopoly capitalism, instead of free market capitalism, in the semiconductor industry. To avoid this consolidation in the semiconductor industry, the existing shares of all major corporations should be given to the employees of these corporations in proportion to their productive contributions. The next step should be to decentralize the fabless companies and make each individual business unit function independently. This means the design engineering team would become an independent business; so would the product engineering team, customer quality engineering, reliability engineering, and so on. The respective businesses would operate at the lower tier or middle tier, depending on their operation as shown in Figure 5.1.

The IDMs, which are currently privately owned and are not able to manufacture the latest technology due to huge capital investments, should also split their fab and fabless businesses in accordance with the previously mentioned approach. The old fabs of IDMs or pure-play foundries that are currently experiencing closure for not being state-of-the-art could function as upper-tier wafer fabs for analog chips. Analog chips do not need cutting-edge transistor technology, and the fabless businesses in these IDMs could be split up into independent businesses to join either the middle tier or the lower tier, based on their business type. Similarly, large tool-manufacturing corporations should be broken into SBUs to enable them to operate as independent small businesses. The wafer fab should give equal opportunities to all SBUs to compete for business to usher in a competitive free market economy. This would encourage new entrepreneurs to start their own businesses in order to provide various engineering and consulting services to the principal wafer fab company to promote innovation. The middle industrial tier of the three-tier model should act as a medium to offer these services to the wafer fab and should also act as the most important sector, which links the end customer (or user of electronic products and services) to the upper and lower tiers of the semiconductor industry.

All engineering service providers involved at the pre-silicon and post-silicon stages should have a healthy competition with one another to usher in a free market economy. This would enable the end customer to get products manufactured at significantly lower costs. Such a decentralization of the fabless businesses would provide the most innovative designs of new products and eliminate any chance of large firms exercising a monopoly power.

Although the quality of products within some of the decentralized economic subsystems would not be as great as those of other economic subsystems, by having bench marking and knowledge sharing through international symposiums, publications, and discussion forums such as Semicon West, EBN, LinkedIn, etc., it would be possible to gradually improve the quality of products and services for the entire global semiconductor industry in all economic subsystems. This is the only way the global semiconductor industry could prosper along with the regional semiconductor industry. In order to boost the development of more fabless SBUs for new entrepreneurs, the local government should help set up SBU associations throughout the economy, which could lease equipment and tools for setting up small businesses like failure-analysis labs, which require significant capital investment. These SBU associations could also offer consultancy to new entrepreneurs at subsidized costs by employing retired industry experts and working on a nonprofit basis. One such organization is SCORE (Service Corps of Retired Executives), which is a resource organization of the Small Business Administration (SBA). SCORE provides mentoring to small businesses in the United States. It has several chapters all across the United States and provides mentoring to small businesses with its network of business knowledge and experience.

Middle Tier—The Employee-sponsored Neo-cooperative Corporate Sector

The middle tier shall include those semiconductor businesses that work directly with end customers. This sector shall include mid-size corporations with a maximum of 500 employees. It would interface directly with end customers, the upper-tier businesses, and the lower-tier businesses. It would consist of cooperatively managed semiconductor companies, where the majority of company assets are owned by company employees. All corporations in this tier should have exchange relationships as a decentralized supply chain. In a decentralized supply chain, individual units make decisions based on local information. In such a system, it becomes easy to incentivize players to act in cooperation, making the entire supply chain efficient.

The sales and marketing division would be able to get feedback on the demands from local customers and draft customer specifications to manufacture customized electronic gadgets, based on the needs of the domestic economy. This middle-industrial-tier team would also interface with lower-tier SBUs, for example, in design engineering for developing customized electronic products as shown in Figure 5.1.

The packaging and assembly of chips would also be done in this tier. This tier would work on voluntary cooperation among its corporations in the middle. However, those corporations that follow the model of employee-sponsored corporations should be given tax incentives to attract the other players in the middle tier to follow the model of employee-owned corporations. Majority shares of these mid-size corporations in the middle tier would be owned by their employees to give them a stake in the success of their businesses. Since the middle tier interfaces with both upper and lower tiers of the economic subsystem, it would be managing the supply and demand of consumer electronics to maintain a balanced economy.

There are many advantages of having the middle tier in the semiconductor industry. If neo-cooperative corporations in this sector notice that customer demand is falling, then they will be able to communicate with the wafer fab at the upper tier and the fabless business unit at the lower tier to avoid overproduction of silicon. This is how the model would make semiconductor manufacturing very sustainable. Both the upper and lower tiers could utilize economic downturns to cut work hours of their employees, to retrain their employees, or to concentrate on R&D activities. In the present global economy, due to the absence of the middle industrial tier, whenever a wafer fab has a stockpiling of inventory, which indicates poor economic demand, unfortunately, the fab lays off its employees.

With this middle tier, the neo-cooperative corporations would be able to adjust the supply and demand of electronics with a cooperative action of producers and consumers. Additionally, the middle tier would provide an accurate real-time estimate of consumer demand, thereby providing feedback to both upper and lower business tiers about customer requirements and demands in order to provide a better customer service.

Another advantage of this three-tier business model is parallel processing, which is very much needed as the industry is progressing to adopt more advanced transistor technology nodes. The middle-level corporate sector would be able to negotiate a good price for pre-silicon and post-silicon services and get the work started simultaneously with shorter life cycles. This way, the manufacturing cycle time could be reduced, and manufacturing costs would decline significantly. Since the majority of corporate shares of this sector are owned by employees, there would be shared growth and prosperity, which would minimize concentration of wealth in the hands of a few.

When the economy grows, the wages of all employees grow, leading to further growth of the overall economy when the employees generate high demand through their wages. The growth of the overall economy grows stock values of the corporations, and hence, the year-over-year profits of all the employees in these corporations, including the CEOs, CFOs, and boards of directors, will also grow steadily. When the economy slows down, the corporations would reduce work hours across the board to avoid job cuts due to layoffs. This way, the problem of unemployment would be permanently solved. Additionally, since the middle tier is an employee-sponsored corporate sector, all majority corporate decisions are made democratically without any influence from nonemployees.

A decentralized supply chain in the middle tier would generate high growth and employment without large-scale migration from rural to urban centers. This would avoid urban congestion and myriad related problems. Such a supply chain also engenders better customer satisfaction by guaranteeing product delivery through an alternative route where the regular supply chain is disrupted by unforeseen events like natural disasters and social or political instability. Additionally, a decentralized supply chain leads to a more cooperative collaboration, rather than competition, between businesses.

This proposed three-tier business model for the global semiconductor industry would wholeheartedly accept automation in the industrial sector. Due to the use of new machines, labor productivity would grow exponentially, as would the supply of goods into the economy. In order to maintain the economic balance, consumer demand would have to match the growth in supply. In such a scenario, the cooperative sector would be able to meet the required production target with fewer work hours but pay its workforce a higher salary in proportion to their higher productivity resulting from the use of machines. This would give sufficient time for employees to pursue further education and vocational training and help the workforce keep up-to-date with the desired skills needed to continue their careers in the ever-progressing and rapidly advancing semiconductor industry.

This business model would make contributions to completely automate production of semiconductor chips from the beginning to the end, which is often referred to as "lights-out fab." The three-tier business model would also lay the groundwork for the establishment of the next generation of ecological fab for sustainable manufacturing. Such a business model would not only lead the fabless semiconductor industry to the next level of innovation and financial success, but it would also act as a model for other capital-intensive industrial sectors in the economy leading to a vibrant growth of both regional and national economies.

Fabless versus IDM

I had authored my first volume *Mass Capitalism* (2014) to let the global semiconductor industry professionals (and particularly the U.S. semiconductor industry professionals) know that the semiconductor industry is headed for a monumental transformation in the very near future due to an upcoming global macroeconomic crisis. Having deep knowledge about the workings of macroeconomics alongwith a decade-long career in the U.S. semiconductor industry working on state-of-the-art tools and technologies, I could foresee what most industry analysts and veterans could not foresee coming to the U.S. economy and its semiconductor industry.

Through my volumes, I have made an attempt to not only raise an alarm for the global semiconductor industry, which is headed in a wrong direction leading to huge problems for the industry at large, but offered free market economic solutions for revival of the semiconductor industry at large. Today, we are observing an increasing consolidation happen in the semiconductor industry and formation of business monopolies through means of eliminating competition in the ecosystem. A healthy competition is essential for preserving innovation in hi-tech industry, and by getting rid of the innovation, the resultant progress of semiconductor industry is truly questionable and so is the continued progress of our knowledge-based economy. Many industry experts talk about the Internet of Things (IoT) as the next big thing, which would lead to an exponential growth of consumer electronic devices and appliances such that it would surpass the combined growth achieved with both computer and mobile revolution. However, I am of the opinion that this exponential growth of IoT market cannot happen in the present macroeconomic environment of industrial monopolies. For IoT revolution to succeed there has to be a true free market economy, a robust growth of small businesses and steady growth in the consumer purchasing power of citizens in the economy.

A debt-based economy, which depends on the growth of consumer debt to drive an economic demand, is absolutely unsustainable in the long run and global macroeconomic crisis since 2008 has made this evident to even a person who has no knowledge about macroeconomics, but in spite of this evidence, the U.S. national debt has grown over $10 trillion since the 2008 financial crisis. Hence, whether it is for letting the IoT revolution to happen, 450-mm silicon wafer transition to occur, Moore's law to progress beyond 10 nm, or for the recovery of global semiconductor industry at large, a good macroeconomic policy and a good monetary policy are essential. Hence, which industrial business model will bring about this IoT revolution—will it be the present form of fabless-foundry business model or the Integrated Device Manufacturers (IDMs) model? The answer is neither, and both these models are a failure from a macroeconomic perspective because IDMs have not supported the growth of small fabless businesses and U.S. trade policies have caused the fabless-foundry business model to contribute to huge trade deficits. The proposed three-tier business model based on free market economic theory of *mass capitalism* is neo-fabless but it is sustainable from a macroeconomic perspective in order to usher in Industry 4.0.

Mass Capitalism Paves the Path for IoT Revolution

The upcoming IoT revolution hopes to extend the end node far beyond the human-centric world to encompass specialized devices with human-accessible interfaces, such as smart home thermostats and blood pressure monitors, and even those which lack human interfaces altogether, including industrial sensors, network-connected cameras, and traditional embedded systems. As IoT grows, the need for real-time scalability to handle dynamic traffic bursts also would increase. Each of those IoT end nodes requires connectivity, processing, and storage, some local, some in the cloud. This means scalability, reliability, security, compliance, and application elasticity to adapt to dynamic requirements and ever-changing workloads.

The proposed three-tier business model mentioned previously would lead to an increase in consumer purchasing power in the economy, thereby increasing the domestic consumer demand. Only when the consumer demand rises through growth in wages, as compared to luring consumers into debt, can the economic demand remain sustainable. When such free market economic reforms become a reality in the U.S. economy as well as the global economy, it would lead to an increased demand for more IoT products like thousands of medical devices in hospitals, smart utility meters, GPS-based location systems, fitness trackers, toll readers, motion detector security cameras, smoke detectors, embedded systems, etc.

As shown in Figure 5.2 subsequently, in order to ensure that IoT revolution is sustainable and leads to a balanced economic growth, where every end node on the Internet, private network, and servers for central systems are able to connect to the private or public cloud, a three-tier business model is highly recommended. In this model, the upper industrial tier would include the servers that need huge capital investments and constant upgrade, which constitutes public and private cloud such as Google Now, Amazon Web Services, etc. The middle industrial tier (as neo-cooperative corporations) to include the public and private broadband Internet providers, networking service providers, computational service providers, Big Data service providers, as well as other software service providers. The lower industrial tier would be the small businesses that can be connected via a network or be individually addressable network

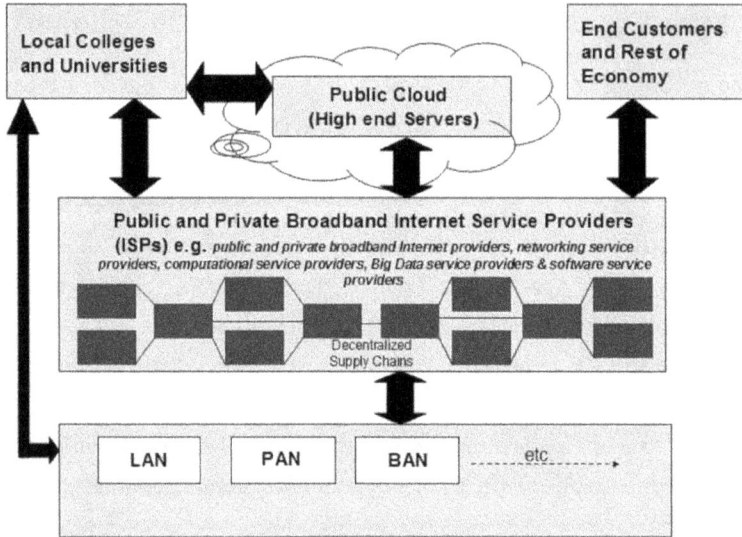

Figure 5.2 A three-tier business model for robust growth of Industry 4.0

Source: Sustaining Moore's Law: Uncertainty Leading to a Certainty of IoT Revolution

(which could be a local area network (LAN), personal area network (PAN), body area network (BAN), etc.).

Low unemployment is key to economic stability and for a robust growth of domestic consumer demand. Only by means of establishing a true free market economy can consumer demand grow in a sustainable way so that the producer of goods would keep investing in better products that cater to the needs of consumers. The IoT specifications also call for lower power devices so that it becomes feasible to have several devices talk to each other in close proximity leading to a strong focus on local economic development. In that regard, decentralization of supply chains becomes essential to bringing about a robust growth of local economies which would further boost the success of IoT revolution, thereby making the semiconductor supply chains more efficient for Industry 4.0.

Conclusion

The fabless-foundry business model has resulted in an increased consolidation in the semiconductor industry and IDM business model has not made it possible to achieve a rapid growth of small businesses in the semiconductor industry. Hence, having a debate between existing fabless-foundry business model and IDM business model is equivalent to debating between which economic system would provide a free market economy for robust growth of small businesses? Will it be crony capitalism or will it be communism? The facts show that neither of the two economic systems has been able to solve the problems of global economy. The solution to the problems faced by global economy is a true free market economy where small businesses prosper in the economy.

In my article published in *LinkedIn*, "Intel Is in Trouble...but so Are TSMC and Samsung," I mentioned that not only the IDMs are making cost cuts but even the foundries catering to fabless semiconductor companies seem to be in trouble. The latter has become evident in an article published in *Forbes*, "Qualcomm Is Breaking up, Already," where it has become obvious that even the largest fabless semiconductor company in the world has faced massive layoffs and will not be able to continue to sustain a progress of Moore's law. This is due to violations of common sense macroeconomics by fabless semiconductor businesses worldwide.

In my proposed three-tier fabless-foundry business model that would lead to a sustainable macroeconomic growth, all the defects of existing fabless-foundry business model have been rectified, defects that have resulted in trade and budget deficits in global economies. Additionally, the power of existing fabless-foundry business model to be able to usher in a growth of small businesses has been preserved. I hope that the global semiconductor industry endorses these proposed free market economic policies as it ushers in the next big thing, the IoT revolution. The sustainability and profitability of this proposed new business model would be useful for every developed economy such as the United States, Germany, France, etc. In addition, it would also help Chinese economy transition to its much-needed consumer-driven economy based on new innovations and driven by a robust consumer demand.

At the same time, my first volume *Mass Capitalism* (2014) would act as a blueprint for establishing semiconductor manufacturing in developing economies like India and to envision Indian prime minister's signature *Make in India* campaign for creating semiconductor manufacturing jobs in India and reduce India's trade deficits from imported electronics.

These projects are presently getting stalled in India due to cancellation of several million dollar projects because of macroeconomic uncertainties; for example, one of India's debt-laden infra-firms, JP Associates has withdrawn its proposal (made back in 2013) to set up a chip plant in partnership with IBM and Israel's Tower Jazz Semiconductor. My volume *Sustaining Moore's Law* (2015) would also act as a blueprint for Indian Prime Minister Narendra Modi's *Digital India* movement to create more service sector jobs in India.

Suggested Readings

[1] Mulay, Apek, *Mass Capitalism: A Blueprint for Economic Revival*, Book Publishers Network, Bothell, WA, 2014.

[2] Mulay, Apek, *Sustaining Moore's Law: Uncertainty Leading to a Certainty of IoT Revolution*, Morgan & Claypool Publishers, San Rafael, CA, 2015.

[3] Mulay, Apek, "*Fabless-Foundry Model v/s Integrated Device Manufacturers Model*", LinkedIn. July 25, 2015. https://www.linkedin.com/pulse/fabless-foundry-model-vs-integrated-device-apekshit-mulay-apek-?trk=mp-reader-card

[4] Mulay, Apek, "*Are Crony Capitalism and Communism Two Sides of Same Coin?*", LinkedIn. April 12, 2014. https://www.linkedin.com/pulse/20140412181124-11893233-are-crony-capitalism-and-communism-two-sides-of-same-coin?trk=mp-reader-card

[5] Singer, Pete, "*A Virtual IDM Concept Can Unite Semiconductor Foundries, Fabless Companies, and Packaging Houses*", Solid State Technology. June 4, 2012. http://electroiq.com/blog/2012/06/virtual-idm-concept-for-foundries-fabless-packaging-houses/

[6] Mulay, Apek, "*Intel Is in Trouble…but so Are TSMC and Samsung*", LinkedIn. July 16, 2015. https://www.linkedin.com/pulse/intel-troublebut-so-tsmc-samsung-apekshit-mulay-apek-?trk=prof-post

[7] Mourdoukoutas, Panos, "*Qualcomm Is Breaking Up, Already*", LinkedIn. July 23, 2015. http://www.forbes.com/sites/panosmourdoukoutas/2015/07/23/qualcomm-is-breaking-up-already/#3a930a442b68

CHAPTER 6

Drivers Proposed by ITRS for *More-than-Moore* and *Beyond* CMOS

Introduction

Over the last half a century, the technological progress of Moore's law has been associated with a reduction in the gate length of transistors on silicon, thereby increasing the speed of operation of integrated circuits (ICs) fabricated on silicon substrate. The international technology roadmap for semiconductors (ITRS) has also provided a roadmap for the semiconductor industry, which was based on the continuous shrinking of the transistors on silicon substrate. However, now the cost of shrinking transistor dimensions is not providing significant return on investment (RoI) any longer. Hence, ITRS has proposed other non-silicon drivers to sustain the profitability and productivity of microelectronics products viz. *More-than-Moore* and *Beyond CMOS*. *More-than-Moore* is a facet of the semiconductor microelectronics that complements the digital part of the integrated systems. More specifically, the *More-than-Moore* approach allows for the non-digital functionalities to be integrated into microelectronic products to improve productivity. These drivers focus on aiding the technological progress by complementing the existing silicon-based ICs with other innovations that are not based on silicon.

While the semiconductor industry has been researching different drivers such as graphene semiconductor, heterojunction transistors, 3D integration, combining silicon with compound semiconductors, newer architectures for CMOS and beyond CMOS, molecular transistors, etc., it is good to have a benchmarking standard with various drivers for the progress of semiconductor industry with *More-than-Moore* and *Beyond CMOS*. The ITRS roadmap has been very successful in setting technological challenges and driving the progress in digital technologies supporting the growth of microelectronics business. The actual list of drivers could be endless and new drivers could emerge in future, but let us take a look at some of these proposed drivers for *More-than-Moore* and *Beyond CMOS*.

Drivers for *More Moore*, *More-than-Moore*, and *Beyond* CMOS

In the following sections of the chapter, we will discuss the various drivers for driving the progress of the semiconductor industry. These drivers are based on some of the recommendations of CATRENE scientific community in their 2011 report "Towards a More-than-Moore Roadmap." Figure 6.1 shows the different industrial sectors catering to the upcoming Industry 4.0 in the form of Internet of things. These drivers include the following:

1. Mobile communication and information
2. Smart automotive
3. Big Data
4. Green/energy technology
5. Medical/health

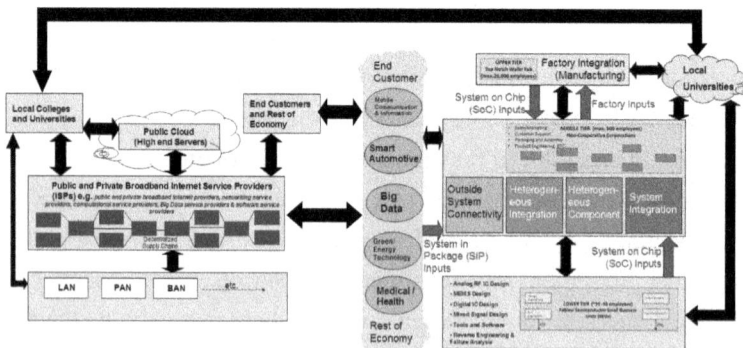

Figure 6.1 *The entire semiconductor ecosystem for envisioning the Internet of things while considering the new drivers for More-than-Moore and Beyond CMOS*

Let us understand each of these sectors and their contributions to various sectors of the economy by catering to variety of demands from consumers. The semiconductor industrial sector would receive the inputs from customers. These inputs would be used by middle-industrial-tier semiconductor companies, which are mostly original equipment manufacturers (OEMs). These companies will provide their specifications to the lower-industrial-tier companies and get their products designed. The inputs to the semiconductor foundry at the upper industrial tier will provide the manufactured wafers. They will be packaged and assembled from companies at the middle industrial tier. Because of the decentralized supply chains at the middle industrial tier, it will be possible to get a much better deal, thereby minimizing costs. The test engineering company at the lower industrial tier will complete the testing and these test results would be used for improving the yield on packaged ICs. The manufactured ICs would be provided to the end customer. The microelectronic chips provided to the customers would be able to connect to the rest of the network with the three-tier business model for Industry 4.0. The model presented in Figure 6-1 will be elaborated further in subsequent chapters and hence does not need to be elaborated here.

It is expected that the non-digital/non-memory part of integrated systems will play an important role in the future. The business model in Figure 6.1 for *More-than-Moore* and *Beyond CMOS* would go well beyond ITRS-proposed drivers and would involve many other actors. Now, let us discuss a few application domains where Industry 4.0 has a way forward.

A Few Application Domains for Industry 4.0

1. **Smart Automotive**

   Modern vehicles make use of up to 80 microcontrollers to create a complex data network. The microelectronic products have found their applications in several electronics modules, such as the following:

   Powertrain Electronics—Engine controllers, transmission controllers, voltage regulators, and other systems controlling engine or driveline of vehicle

   Entertainment Electronics—AM/FM radio, satellite radio, onboard video entertainment system

Safety and Convenience System—Airbag sensors, climate controls, security and access controls, antilock braking systems

Vehicle and Body Controls—To manage suspension, traction, and power steering

In-Cabin Information Systems—Instrument clusters, trip computers, telematic products

Non-embedded Sensors—Speed sensors, temperature sensors, fluid-level sensors, etc.

On a component level, the following areas need to be addressed:

Integrated Sensors—Measuring pressure (manifold air pressure, fuel, occupant detection, tire, and airbags)

Gas/Chemical Sensors—In-cabin air quality, monitoring exhaust gas composition, and oil quality

Actuator/Valves—To detect fuel injection

Optical/Infrared Sensors—For in-car local area networks (LANs), heating, ventilation and air conditioning control, occupant sensing, night vision, and in-vehicle displays

Radar-based Sensors—Backup aid, blind-spot detection, adaptive cruise control

2. **Wearable Healthcare**

The advancements in microelectronics are of paramount importance in ensuring that the new wearable healthcare devices are smaller and more comfortable to wear, robust against motion artifact, power efficient, intelligent as well as able to communicate with user. Wearable healthcare is proposed to reduce the healthcare costs through prevention, monitoring, and e-health.

As explained in subsequent sections of this chapter, when the economy shifts toward a more collaborative patient-centered care, the need for interoperable and low-cost devices and services increases. The sensors used in wearable health needs to incorporate an increasing functionality and intelligence and be able to communicate with other devices and wider health services through the IoT platform.

The important advancements in microelectronics for wearable healthcare can be grouped into following components:

Sensors and Circuitry—Sensitive sensors for accurately monitoring relevant signals

Digital Signal Processing and Digital Signal Processors—Reducing power consumption and allowing intelligence to be embedded in wearable health system

Integration Technologies—Integrating electronic components while maintaining flexibility and stretchability of devices

Memory—The memory could be either local or it could be external, in which case the data must be transmitted electronically

Power Management—For power management, both ultra-low power consumption and energy harvesting technology are essential

Radio Technologies—Real-time monitoring and alerting using wireless communication

Body/Electronics Interface—It is necessary to capture the relevant body signals at required quality. In case of electrical measurements, it could be electrodes with or without contact gel.

The major application domains for wearable/health care products are as follows:

Monitoring—Making a correct diagnosis from long-term, diagnostically relevant data monitoring. This long-term data can be recorded and provided offline for making a correct diagnosis. They do not have an on-board intelligence for decision-making.

Prevention—To perform cautious monitoring of certain disorder in order to provide an alarm to protect or prevent the onset of disorder. They require an on-board intelligence to provide an alert to the user or automatic feedback and hence require advanced digital signal processing (DSP) capabilities.

Closed Loop—Automatic detection of an adverse event and automatically providing an output to overcome that adverse event. They require an on-board intelligence to provide an alert to the user or automatic feedback and hence require advanced DSP capabilities.

Spot Check—Whenever desired, the user could measure a body function thus requiring less-stringent power consumption as compared to the above three.

3. **Biochips and Lab-on-chips**

There have been great efforts in the fields of biology, chemistry, and engineering to pursue the advantages of miniaturization for cheaper, better, and faster devices that could be used in life sciences as bio-microsystems, which encompass a variety of devices, depending on the technology used or for a targeted application making use of biosensors.

The following are main areas of focus where biosensors technology is strictly related to the evolution of microelectronics industry:

Parallelism—As learned from the micro-electronics industry, miniaturization can lead to massive parallelism, and this could help in carrying out several reactions in parallel. This could be very useful in the manufacture of pharmaceuticals.

Reduced Reagent Consumption—As these compounds are very expensive, performing tests by reducing the volume of reaction vessel by orders of magnitude is certainly a direct benefit. Also, cost reduction for screening compound libraries that are used by pharmaceutical companies is another benefit of miniaturization.

Speed/Throughput—Miniaturization not only has an advantage in increasing the speed to improve performance parameters but also has advantages for experimentation in physics, such as mass transfer or heat transfer.

Functional Integration—Miniaturization would enable complex multistep tasks to be performed quickly and cheaply, which traditionally require a lot of different machines.

4. **Mobile Communication and Information**

The striking speed of the exponential growth in the cell phone use and the rapid growth of mobile communications has caught the attention of several semiconductor companies. With a powerful smartphone in their hands, people are now empowered with a multipurpose tool like never before. Today, the semiconductor industry is making great efforts to increase the capability of chips on cell phones, increase computation power, lower power consumption, as well as improve power management in smartphones of the next generation. Several wireless communication protocols and technologies exist today that are used to meet the range, power consumption, and data rate for different applications. Today, most smartphones come enabled with Bluetooth for communication over short distances and are able to operate over one or more wireless cellular networks like GSM, CDMA, or GPRS. Both Wi-Fi and WiMAX (Wide Interoperability for Microwave Access) based on 802.11 standard have revolutionized the use of smartphones.

When it comes to Industry 4.0, several wireless standards are still under development that would facilitate wearable sensor networks, specifically targeting the requirements for low power, privacy and quality of service, coexistence, as well as compatibility. The low-power requirements call for ushering in a local economy and *mass capitalism*-based free market economy will usher in a strong local economy that is focused on increasing consumer purchasing power in the economy, thereby driving an economic demand. For wireless communication at shorter distance, Bluetooth, Zigbee, and IEEE 802.15 communications are mostly used. The goal of Bluetooth has been to provide a flexible cable replacement technology at low cost, which is insensitive to any interference and is compatible with different products from different brands but has lower power consumption. Bluetooth's progress has been toward higher data rate or lower power (and hence a lower bandwidth).

One of the important necessities of wireless health monitors is connectivity, to a remote patient monitoring system, personal data storage system, or other network device. Hence, a robust mobile communication infrastructure is equally important as are the devices needed for monitoring. Further, mobile phones can act as a gateway between personal area networks (PAN) and outside network, thus creating data traffic. As shown in Figure 6.1, this data can be transferred to the Cloud for storage or can be transferred to a doctor via the broadband infrastructure after performing data analysis. In this way, mobile communication and information could play an important role in the management of personal wireless sensor networks, mobile phone-centric data collection, signal processing, preventive wellness history presentation for self-care, and integration of wellness data of patient with the database.

In case of wireless communication, there could be advances to heterogeneous semiconductors in order to improve the speed of operation. RF analog microelectronics on different semiconductor substrate materials like GaAs, Si, GaN, etc. would drive the growth of *More-than-Moore* and *Beyond CMOS*.

5. **Big Data Analytics**

   Big data analytics is an advanced analytical technique to work on terabytes and zegabytes of data, which could be either structured or unstructured, streaming or batch, etc. This goes beyond the capability of traditional relational databases to capture, manage, and process data. The data can arrive from either web, social media, log files, networks, transactional applications, sensors, or other devices. Big data analytics helps analysts, teachers, and business leaders make much more informed decision using data that was previously inaccessible or unusable. This provides businesses an approach to analyze previously untapped resources through use of advanced analytic techniques such as text analytics, machine analytics, predictive analytics, data mining, statistics, natural language processing, etc.

   In order to perform analytics over such a large quantity of data, Big Data analytics capability may include the following:

   Data Management and Warehouse: This gains database performance across multiple workloads while lowering administration, storage, development, and server costs. It also realizes extreme speed with capabilities optimized for analytic workloads such as deep analytics, and benefit from workload-optimized systems that can be up and running in hours.

   Server: Helps bring the power of servers with application accelerators, analytics, visualization, development tools, performance, and security features.

   Stream Computing: Efficiently delivering real-time analytic processing on constantly changing data in motion, enabling descriptive and predictive analytics to support real-time decisions, continuously capturing and analyzing all data, thereby storing less data and analyzing more data in order to make better and faster decisions.

   Content Management: Enabling comprehensive content, life cycle, and document management with cost-effective controls of existing and new types of content with scale, security, and stability.

   Integration and Governance: Integrating, understanding, managing, and governing data during its life cycle.

The above-mentioned applications would include a variety of processing and storage microelectronics to achieve the corresponding functions. Hence, big data analytics would lead to an explosive growth in the microelectronics industry while ushering in Industry 4.0. As the requirement for faster data analytics increases, so would the need for 3D integration, silicon-on-insulator, multipackage integration, high electron mobility transistor (HEMT), as well as newer architectures such as distributed computing, improved software efficiencies, etc. drive the progress of *More-than-Moore* and *Beyond CMOS*. Efficient parallel programming as well as multicore scaling shall also play an important role in driving further growth of faster data analytics with *More-than-Moore* and *Beyond CMOS*.

Beyond CMOS Drivers for *More-than-Moore* and *Beyond* CMOS

The following are some of the drivers for *More-than-Moore* and *Beyond CMOS* when it comes to "Beyond CMOS" technologies:

1. **Tunneling FET**

    A tunneling FET (TFET) makes use of the principle of quantum tunneling of electrons. With the continued progress of Moore's law, as chipmakers have squeezed ever more transistors onto a chip, transistors have gotten smaller, and the distances between different transistor regions have decreased. Therefore, the electronic barriers that were once thick enough to block current have now become so thin that electrons can barrel right through them. TFET switches "on" and "off" by changing the likelihood of electrons on one side of the barrier to make it or not make it to the other side. In case of classical electrodynamics, an electron would bounce back from the energy barrier if its energy did not exceed the barrier height. However, in case of quantum mechanics, electrons have a finite probability of passing through the barrier. The thinner the barrier width for electron tunneling, the higher is the probability that such an event could occur. Instead of raising or lowering the physical barrier between the source and drain as like a MOSFET, TFET uses a gate to control the effective electrical thickness of the barrier and thus the probability of electrons tunneling through it. Thus, although the current-control mechanism in the TFET is new, the device bears a strong resemblance to MOSFET.

2. **Graphene p–n Junction**

The advantage of making use of graphene as compared with other semiconductor material is that graphene functions as a gapless semiconductor, which means that it has a zero band gap voltage between the valence and conduction band. As a consequence, it is easy to tune between any n-type semiconductor (electrons are the main charge carriers) or p-type (holes are the main charge carriers) semiconductor material. When a positive gate voltage is applied to graphene, it shifts the Fermi level into the conduction band, thereby creating a p-type semiconductor. Similarly, when a negative gate voltage is applied to graphene, it will lower the Fermi level to the valence band, thereby making holes the dominant carriers.

This property exhibited by graphene means that a single sheet of graphene can function as a p–n junction by applying a positive voltage to an electrode on one side of the graphene sheet and negative voltage on the other side of the sheet through electrodes. The applied voltage shifts the Fermi levels in those regions and creates the junction. Before the above-mentioned use of graphene was researched by some researchers based in Canada, there were attempts made to manufacture single-sheet junctions that made use of a top gate in conjunction with a bottom gate. These techniques made use of the substrate as the bottom gate, which lowered the Fermi level of the entire sheet. A single top gate could be used to raise the Fermi level locally. However, in order to overcome the bottom gate potential, the top gate voltage needed to be raised is high enough and that caused damage to graphene or its $I–V$ characteristics started showing high nonlinearity. However, when a single voltage is applied locally, comparatively very low voltages are necessary. This preserved the material and its linear characteristics. Graphene has amazing electronic properties, which could make it a suitable replacement for silicon. However, there is not an easy method for large-scale processing of graphene-based materials, so this may take a considerable amount of time before we could start seeing graphene-based computers on the shelf at Best Buy, Fry's electronics, etc.

3. Spintronics and Orbitronics

Spintronics makes use of a property of electrons called "spin" in order to produce a novel kind of current that ICs can process as information. "Spin" refers to how an electron rotates on its axis, which is very similar to the rotation of the Earth about its axis. In 2003, Professor Zhang demonstrated at the University of Tokyo that producing and manipulating a current of allied electron spins by means of an electric field would not involve any losses of heat. This is called "spintronics."

In his research, Professor Zhang discovered that "spintronics" does not work well for lighter atoms like silicon, which are used in the semiconductor industry. However, researchers have shown that silicon can be used in a related technology, dubbed "orbitronics." Both spintronics and orbitronics make use of a physical quantity called "angular momentum," which is essentially the property of every mass that moves about its axis. In a conventional IC, electric current is nothing but a flow of negatively charged electrons. Similarly, orbital current is the flow of electrons with their angular momenta aligned in an orbital circuit.

If an electron is pushed forward in an electric field, the orbital current is perpendicular to the electric current. Orbital current will have its angular momentum perpendicular to the direction of current but will not carry any charge. Thus, orbitronics will still preserve silicon as a useful material as there will not be significant losses due to heat at room temperature. Research into spintronics and developing a commercial transistor application has been going on for more than 15 years, but none has yet made it into production. Appealingly, the voltage needed to drive them is very small, around 10–20 mV, hundreds of times lower than what is needed for a conventional transistor. When transistors are operated at such low voltages, the problem of heat dissipation could be easily solved.

Conclusion

This chapter touches upon a few of the drivers proposed by ITRS. The scope of this chapter is vast as there are so many other sectors of the economy that would have contribution to *More-than-Moore* and *Beyond*

CMOS and thus could fill several more pages of this book. There are several working groups of ITRS working on these different drivers for *More-than-Moore* and *Beyond CMOS*. However, the purpose of this chapter was to provide the reader with a brief introduction to the possible ways in which Industry 4.0 and *More-than-Moore* can bring about the next microelectronics revolution.

However, all the suggested drivers proposed by ITRS only contribute to the supply of goods into the economy. There has to be an equally good demand for those goods for Industry 4.0 to become possible as well as *More-than-Moore* and *Beyond CMOS* to be able to drive the growth of semiconductor industry. Without any macroeconomic reforms to usher in an economic demand in proportion to the rising supply of manufactured electronics, not only is the future of Industry 4.0 questionable but even further progress of the semiconductor industry beyond 50 years of the progress of Moore's law is truly questionable.

Suggested Readings

[1] Wolfgang, Arden, Brillouet Michael, Cogez Patrick, Graef Mart, Huizing Bert, Mahnkopf Reinhard, Pelka Joachim, Pfeiffer Jens-Uwe, Rouzaud Andre, Tartagni Marco, Chris Van Hoof, Wagner Joachim, "*Towards a More-than-Moore Roadmap*", Report from the CATRENE Scientific Community. November 8, 2011.

[2] Mulay, Apek, *Mass Capitalism: A Blueprint for Economic Revival*, Book Publishers Network, Bothell, WA, 2014.

[3] Mulay, Apek, *Sustaining Moore's Law: Uncertainty Leading to a Certainty of IoT Revolution*, Morgan & Claypool Publishers, San Rafael, CA, 2015.

[4] Liu, Jingping, Safieddin Safavi-Naeini, Dayan Ban, "*Fabrication and measurement of graphene p-n junction with two top gates*", Electronic Letters, Vol. 50, No. 23, pp 1724–1726, November 6, 2014. DOI:10.1049/el.2014.3061. http://phys.org/news/2014-11-single-sheet-graphene-p-n-junction-gates.html#jCp

[5] Seabaugh, Alan, "*The Tunneling Transistor*", IEEE Spectrum. September 30, 2013. http://spectrum.ieee.org/semiconductors/devices/the-tunneling-transistor

[6] Orienstein, David, "*New Spin on Semiconductors: 'Orbitronics' Advances Silicon-Based Computing*", Stanford Report. September 27, 2005. http://news.stanford.edu/news/2005/september28/orbitron-092805.html

CHAPTER 7

Sustaining the Progress of *More-than-Moore* and *Beyond* CMOS with *Mass Capitalism*

Introduction

In Chapter 4 of this volume, we analyzed all the information provided by ITRS for driving the growth of the semiconductor industry for the next 15 years, which can be considered the roadmap for the semiconductor industry. After analyzing all the information presented by ITRS for driving *More-than-Moore* and *Beyond CMOS*, I would like to reiterate that the ITRS has failed to provide any solution to the diminishing consumer demand in the global economy, in spite of acknowledging the fact that multifaceted public consumer has become an influential driver of the semiconductor industry because of an ever-increasing demand of custom functionality in commercial electronic products. In addition, the ITRS has not taken into consideration the macroeconomics of the semiconductor manufacturing business in proposing its business model for 2020 and beyond. Furthermore, ITRS also falls short of providing any explanation for how to go about measuring the contribution made by the different proposed drivers toward growth of the semiconductor industry. In this chapter, we will understand how progress of Moore's law could be sustained with a proper macroeconomic policy that restores a free market economy. We will also envision the ideas for *More-than-Moore* and *Beyond CMOS* in this chapter.

Proposed Innovative Business Model for the Semiconductor Industry to Sustain Progress of *More-than-Moore* and *Beyond* CMOS

In *Mass Capitalism* (2014) and *Sustaining Moore's Law* (2015), I propose an innovative business model for the global semiconductor industry and the Internet of things (IoT) that addresses most of the questions that have been left unanswered by the ITRS. In fact, the proposed three-tier business model, as discussed in Chapter 5, would ensure a long-term sustainability and profitability of the semiconductor business while sustaining the continued progress of Moore's law as well as usher in the IoT revolution. The advantage of the proposed new business model is that it takes the merits of both Integrated Device Manufacturer (IDM) and fabless-foundry business models and rectifies their flaws, which ensures macroeconomic sustainability.

As this chapter deals with a top-down hierarchy of the semiconductor industry, we will consider the benefits of my three-tier business model proposed only for the semiconductor industry in order to address those questions that have been left unanswered by the ITRS. Here, we are not going to discuss the three-tier business model for ushering in IoT revolution as discussed in my 2015 volume. However, we will observe how the complete Industry 4.0 ecosystem looks like with drivers for *More-than-Moore* and *Beyond CMOS*. We will also learn about how the proposed new drivers for Moore's law can fit into this new business model thereby envisioning the contribution of each of the ITRS's drivers toward the progress of the semiconductor industry.

While the IDM business model has helped create more domestic manufacturing jobs and protected the intellectual property (IP), the fabless-foundry business model ushered in a new era of growth of several small fabless semiconductor businesses. This fabless revolution has over the years enabled creation of several small design facilities, testing facilities and failure analysis laboratories, etc. In addition, there has been a pretty robust collaboration between fabless companies and their foundries. However, the fabless business model since its inception has ignored the macroeconomic policies that have resulted in increasing trade and budget deficits due to globalization of semiconductor manufacturing.

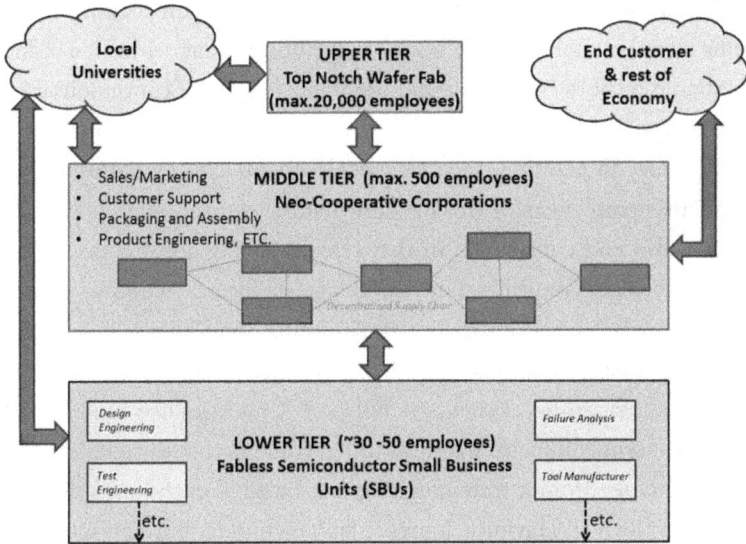

Figure 7.1 **A three-tier business model for the global semiconductor industry**

Source: Mass Capitalism: A Blueprint for Economic Revival (2014). [Repeated from Chapter 5 for convenience of the reader]

The fabless-foundry business model also led to the problem of counterfeit electronics entering the supply chains of developed economies where, as the General Accounting Office (GAO) estimated, approximately 40 percent of U.S. DoD (Department of Defense) supply chain is filled with defective or counterfeit electronic goods. In order to ensure profitability of any project, a proper macroeconomic policy is essential because only a good macroeconomic policy ensures the health of the macroeconomy. A proper macroeconomic policy ushers in healthy growth of both supply and demand, which acts as an engine for the economic growth.

The supply of goods comes from the productivity of workforce and the demand for these goods comes from the wages of the workforce. A free market economic policy that ensures a steady growth in supply and demand should adopt a policy such that wages of workforce keeps track with workers' productivity. Such a policy ensures that there exists a sustainable demand for manufactured goods in order to ensure their consumption. Only when there is a healthy demand for the manufactured goods, do more investments come into the economy in order to get a good return on investments (RoI). Semiconductor manufacturing being a very capital-intensive business, the business model for the industry should be both sustainable and profitable in spite of continuous ever-increasing capital investments that are needed for driving the progress of Moore's law. In addition, the macroeconomic policies should usher in a competitive capitalism or free markets that benefit not only the producers but also end consumers. In that regard, having a domestic fabless-foundry business model is more advantageous for any economy as long as all fabless businesses get their manufacturing done from only domestic foundries, thereby eliminating any trade deficits resulting from offshoring of manufacturing, design, assembly, etc. Countries like India, which lack IP for semiconductor manufacturing, could license this manufacturing technology from a technologically advanced country until they develop their own IP. Having a domestic fabless-foundry business model for every economy is critical in order to reduce the dependence on imported electronics, which contributes to trade deficits and eventually causes a devaluation of country's currency and depreciates the standard of living of citizens.

Every economy goes through waxing and waning macroeconomic cycles of nature. A more detailed explanation as well as an impact of these macroeconomic cycles on the semiconductor industry business models have been presented in Chapter 5, "Macroeconomic Cycles and Business Models for the Progress of Moore's Law," in my volume *Sustaining Moore's Law*(2015). In order to have a true free market economy where the role of government is small and intervention of the government into the economy is minimal, having a collaborative business model as well as formulating proper macroeconomic policies is critical. The business model of semiconductor industry should minimize the problem of unemployment during economic downturns. Only in such a situation would it be possible to have low income taxes on citizens of a country; else taxes would have to be raised from the employed in order to pay for unemployment insurance benefits of the unemployed. If there is a huge unemployment during an economic downturn, the government has to spend money for paying unemployment benefits to the laid-off workers. In an economic downturn, the government could also give tax cuts to businesses in order to revive the economy. But, in either case, the budget deficits rise as taxpaying citizens cannot pay their fair share of taxes and so does the government spending rises in order to finance those deficits. These policies indirectly hurt the value of currency and raise the country's national debt. Hence, in order to minimize the size of the government and to have lower intervention of government in the economy, it is essential to formulate proper macroeconomic policies that would avoid huge unemployment during economic downturns.

Taking this into consideration, an innovative three-tier business model has been presented in Figure 7.1, which would not only provide a more collaborative business model but would also minimize the problems of huge unemployment during economic downturns. This is possible with the presence of a middle-industrial tier (MIT) that interacts directly with the end customer and rest of the economy. Due to an absence of this MIT in present economy, there is no monitoring of slowdown in consumer demand resulting in excess supply and poor demand, leading to layoffs in the manufacturing and service sectors. In addition, this business model ensures a much better integration by having a diverse set of products from different design teams giving an added flexibility to the businesses in the MIT in order to manufacture customized multifaceted products for customers. There are many more benefits of this business model such as getting support from local government in order to keep this capital-intensive semiconductor manufacturing business sustainable while still ensuring that there is a minimal government intervention into the economy.

A top-notch wafer fab needs an investment larger than what is needed for a nuclear reactor. In 2013, the cost of building the next-generation wafer fab was estimated at over $10 billion. The suitability of the location of a wafer fab depends upon the ready availability of all necessary raw materials needed for manufacturing. The local government should build the necessary infrastructure, like a domestic or international airport, good transportation facilities, good infrastructure, etc., for a smooth delivery of the goods to end customers. This would ensure the growth of smaller and medium-size businesses that would cater to that fab. Any infrastructure investment would be a long-term investment to attract other businesses.

In order to have a balanced economy, the official monetary policy should be such that wages keep up with labor productivity. Since workers' wages contribute to consumer demand and workers' productivity contributes to the supply of goods, when wages catch up with productivity, supply and demand grow and fall together. Hence, it is important that company profits are first shared among the employees in proportion to their productive contributions and then later with outside investors. In order to ensure that wages catch up with productivity, there should be special incentives—a share of the profits—offered to highly productive and innovative employees. The remaining profits, if any, should be shared with the private non-employee investors as return on their investments. It is very important for an economy to first ensure that wages catch up with productivity to maintain a rational distribution of wages. This would also eliminate any economic imbalance that might result from huge wage disparities.

In this way, the proposed three-tier business model would ensure an increased collaboration across the entire semiconductor industry, thereby driving the growth of the overall industry and its affiliated industries. Another advantage of this model is increasing the consumer's purchasing power and hence being able to benefit the overall economy by means of transitioning to an ever-increasing diameter of silicon wafers, thereby increasing the profitability for the manufacturers as well as reducing the costs of products for end consumers. In fact, 450-mm transition is a huge step forward that could be adopted by the global semiconductor industry in order to come out of its ongoing economic stagnation, and the proposed three-tier business model would also help the semiconductor industry in this transition process by ensuring a good RoI through continuous growth in consumer demand.

Envisioning *More-than-Moore* and *Beyond* CMOS for the Semiconductor Industry

In this section, we will discuss envisioning the ideas proposed by ITRS for *More-than-Moore* and *Beyond CMOS* so that not only does the progress become sustainable but also becomes feasible to measure growth of the semiconductor industry. With the growth of the semiconductor industry measured by the progress of Moore's law since 1965 until recently, there has been predictability when it comes to the progress of the industry to its next technological node driving investments into the economy in order to get a better RoI. When there exist multiple drivers for the progress of the semiconductor industry for *More-than-Moore* and *Beyond CMOS*, there has to be a conclusive understanding of how progress of the industry is to be measured in order to get a better RoI.

As elaborated above, there are a few benefits of the proposed three-tier business model based on the free market macroeconomic theory of *mass capitalism*, and this model will play a significant role in sustaining the progress of Moore's law by means of increasing consumer purchasing power in the economy. Now, let me also explain how this proposed three-tier business model would also sustain the ITRS proposed drivers for *More-than-Moore* and *Beyond CMOS*.

Let me briefly explain how the various drivers proposed by ITRS would sustain this progress of *More-than-Moore* and *Beyond CMOS*. As shown in Figure 7.2, the ever-increasing consumer demand will drive the demand for latest electronic gadgets and System-in-Package (SiP) inputs would cater to that demand for customized gadgets, by means of obtaining those inputs from the prospective customers. The semiconductor companies that will form the MIT will mostly be the original equipment manufacturers (OEMs), which would employ those semiconductor industry professionals who primarily interact directly with the end consumer or end user of the product.

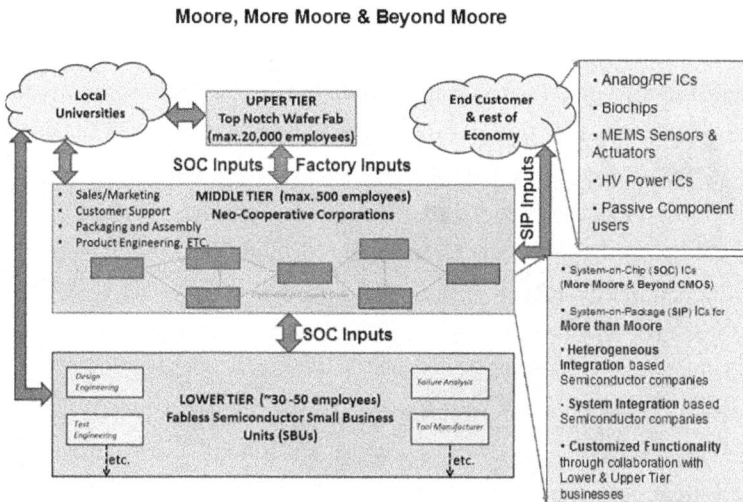

Figure 7.2 How the driving forces for Industry 4.0 as proposed by ITRS fit into the three-tier business model based on mass capitalism

Depending on the inputs received from their consumers, the semi-conductor industry professionals, at MIT, will draft specifications for the products used in nondigital functionalities involving RF analog ICs, biochips, MEMS actuators and sensors, high-volume power ICs, passive components, etc. that will be combined into SiP driving the *More-than-Moore* path. The *More-than-Moore* and *Beyond CMOS* inputs will come from both lower and upper industrial tiers as companies at MIT perform the function of electronic design automation (EDA), juggling with different customized designs from lower industrial tier (LIT) as per the customized functionality ordered from the end customer. The SoC inputs for these new designs would come from the upper and lower industrial tiers, which will provide SoC inputs for both circuit design and manufacturing process. Thereby, it will be at the MIT where a heterogeneous integration of different designs and manufacturing processes will take place.

While the OEMs at MIT will consist of few experts from different domains including design, process, failure analysis, etc. for the sake of getting the work done from both LIT and upper industrial tier (UIT), the manufacturing will be done primarily at UIT, and small businesses at LIT will provide innovative designs, testing tools and methodologies, failure analysis, reverse engineering facilities, etc. that would be available for use by the MIT. By means of segregating the key engineering functions at different industrial tiers, it would become easier for the semiconductor companies at MIT to get a real-time feedback based on the inputs in the economy. This will also help these semiconductor companies to meet their consumer demand by interfacing with the UIT and LIT. During economic downturns, the MIT could provide a feedback to both upper and lower industrial tiers in order to avoid overproduction of electronics and thus avoid layoffs. Having small and medium-sized businesses in the lower and middle industrial tiers would usher n a competitive capitalism or free markets in the semiconductor industry. For this model to work efficiently and remain as a free market business enterprise, anti-trust laws have to be strictly enforced in order to avoid Mergers and Acquisitions (M&As) between profitable firms, which result in the formation of business monopolies, eventually destroying the competitive capitalism or free markets. Larger size of a business and elimination of competition puts those large-sized businesses in a position to start controlling the prices rather than let the market forces control the prices of electronics. In this way, by means of ushering in true free markets, such policies would also help put a check on the ability of any business to be able to control prices of consumer electronics and other electronic products in Industry 4.0.

The progress of the semiconductor industry will be measured by the ability of this three-tier business model to grow consumer demand in the economy by means of following a monetary policy such that wages are in line with employee productivity. There are several other macroeconomic policies such as the "minimum necessities" and "maximum amenities," which will be discussed in Chapter 9, which will help drive the consumer demand in the economy. When the consumer demand starts growing steadily, new businesses are created in the economy catering to the growing consumer demand. This creates a multiplier effect, driving the economic growth. In this way, the proposed three-tier business model will ensure that global semiconductor industry will prosper for years to come, driving the growth of the knowledge-based economy providing a predictable RoI for businesses and thus driving more investments into the economy. In addition, when these ideas are adopted while ushering in the fourth industrial revolution, the resulting industrial revolution would become both sustainable and profitable in the long run.

The Driving Forces for *More-than-Moore* and *Beyond* CMOS

Let us now try to analyze how the driving forces for *More-than-Moore* and *Beyond CMOS* fit into the proposed business model so that it becomes easier to not only implement these drivers but also gauge their contributions to progress.

As shown in Figure 7.3, the inputs from different sectors in an economy that are part of Industry 4.0 will contribute as inputs for driving the growth of semiconductor industry.

These sectors include the following:

1. Mobile communication and information
2. Smart automotive
3. Big Data

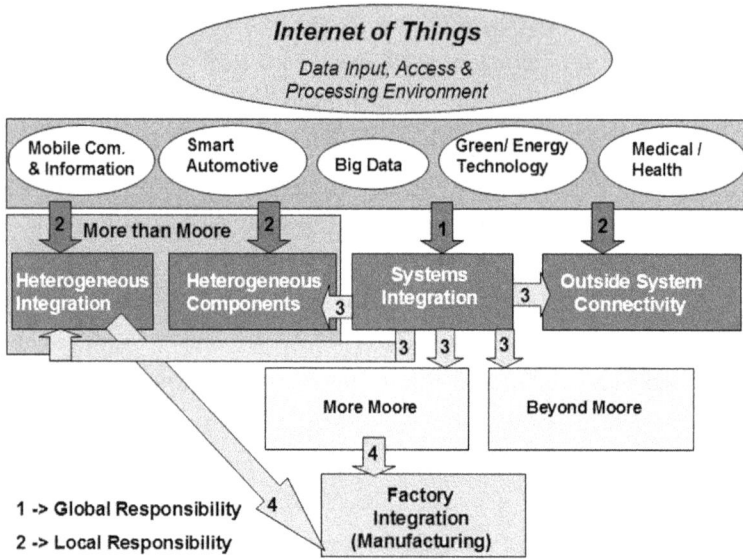

Figure 7.3 An assessment of driving forced for Industry 4.0 through More-than-Moore and Beyond CMOS drivers

Source: ITRS, Feb 2015. (Repeated from Chapter 4 for convenience of the reader)

4. Green energy/technology
5. Medical/health

While Figure 7.2 shows where most of these components fit into the semiconductor industry business model, now let us see how the semiconductor business model for ushering Industry 4.0 would look like as shown in Figure 7.4.

As can be clearly understood from Figure 7.4, the MIT is the most important sector of the economy and has a significantly important role to play for driving *More-than-Moore* and *Beyond CMOS*. It receives the System on Chip (SoC) inputs from the different fabless businesses at LIT as well as process inputs from the UIT. The businesses at MIT get their SiP inputs from the different businesses that cater to Industry 4.0 as well as provide the factory inputs for getting manufacturing done from MIT.

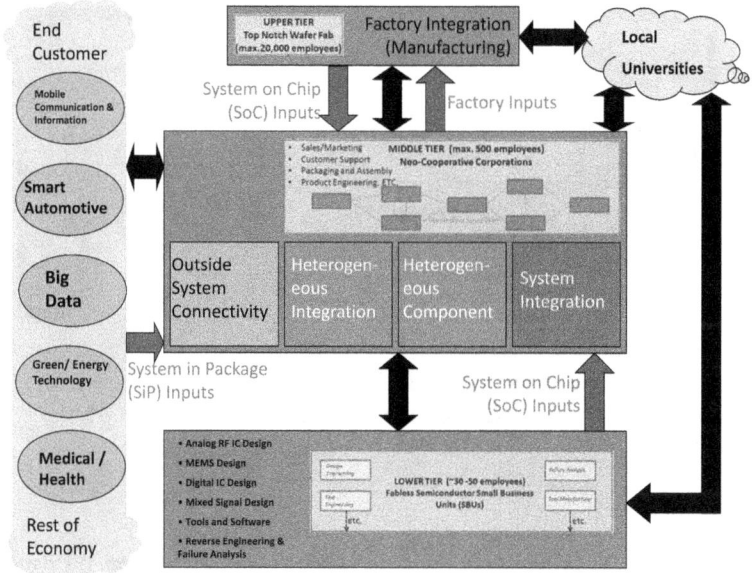

Figure 7.4 An illustration of how the various drivers as proposed by ITRS for More-than-Moore and Beyond CMOS fit into the proposed three-tier business model for the global semiconductor industry

The businesses at MIT would be the OEMs and these OEMs at MIT will have four different types of companies that would have an exchange relationship in the form of decentralized supply chain. Based on these operations, the OEMs will be categorized as follows:

1. Companies dealing with heterogeneous integration
2. Companies dealing with heterogeneous components
3. Companies dealing with system integration
4. Companies that deal with the outside system connectivity

In this way, by means of having *More-than-Moore* and *Beyond CMOS* drivers in a three-tier business model, the global semiconductor industry will continue on a path of sustainable progress as explained in my previous two volumes. Figure 7.5 shows how the entire Industry 4.0 eco-system looks like with *More-than-Moore* and *Beyond CMOS* drivers.

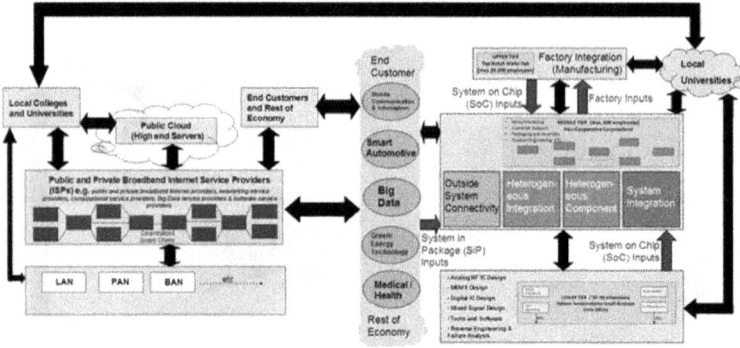

Figure 7.5 The entire semiconductor ecosystem for envisioning the
Internet of things considering the new drivers for More-than-Moore
and Beyond CMOS.(This figure has been repeated from Chapter 6 for
convenience of the reader.)

Other Advantages of This Three-Tier Business Model

Since its inception in 1965, Moore's law has provided a predictable business model for the global semiconductor industry, which led to high investments into the economy in order to reap a greater RoI. Hence, when
the semiconductor industry plans adopting More-than-Moore and Beyond
CMOS as its drivers, it has to be ensured that there is a predictable business model for the industry for investments to come into the economy.
As published by the ITRS chair, it takes 12–15 years of incubation time
for newer technologies to show their impact on the progress of Moore's
law. However, the impact of the three-tier business model in driving the
growth of global semiconductor industry by sustaining the progress of
Moore's law will be observed immediately without much delay. In fact,
this model will break the usual cycles of boom and bust, thereby keeping the trajectory of semiconductor industry on a path of continuous
progress.

A decentralized supply chain at MIT would generate high growth and
employment without large-scale migration from rural to urban areas. This
would avoid urban congestion and myriad related problems. Such supply
chains also engender a better customer satisfaction by means of guaranteeing product delivery through an alternative route in cases where the
regular supply chain gets disrupted by unforeseen events such as natural
disasters and social or political instability.

It should be noted that this three-tier business model for the global semiconductor industry would wholeheartedly accept automation in the industrial sector. With the use of new electronic gadgets, the labor productivity would grow exponentially and hence the supply of goods into the economy would also grow. In order to maintain an economic balance, consumer demand would have to match the growth in supply. In such a scenario the MIT sector would be able to meet the required production target with fewer work hours due to automation but pay its workforce a higher salary in proportion to their higher productivity resulting from the use of machines. This would give sufficient leisure time for employees to pursue further education and vocational training, and help the workforce to keep up-to-date with the desired skills needed to continue their careers in the ever-progressing and rapidly advancing semiconductor industry.

This business model would make significant contributions to completely automate the production of semiconductor chips from its beginning to the end which is often referred to as "Lights-out Fab." Such a business model would not only lead the global semiconductor industry to its next level of innovation and financial success, but would also act as a model for other sectors in the economy leading to a vibrant growth of regional and national economies. In this way, the three-tier business model can envision the *More-than-Moore* and *Beyond CMOS* drivers to sustain the progress of today's knowledge-based economy.

Suggested Readings

[1] Mulay, Apek, *Mass Capitalism: A Blueprint for Economic Revival*, Book Publishers Network, Bothell, WA, 2014.
[2] Mulay, Apek, *Sustaining Moore's Law: Uncertainty Leading to a Certainty of IoT Revolution*, Morgan & Claypool Publishers, San Rafael, CA, 2015.
[3] Gargini, Paolo, "*ITRS—Past, Present and Future.*" February 2015.

CHAPTER 8

Measurement of the Progress for *More-than-Moore* and *Beyond* CMOS

Introduction

In the previous chapter, we discussed an innovative three-tier business model for the global semiconductor industry. We also observed how the various drivers for *More-than-Moore* and *Beyond CMOS* would fit into this innovative business model. The progress of Moore's law provided a well-defined goal for the measurement of progress, thereby driving the progress of global semiconductor industry. In this way, the business model for growth of global semiconductor industry based on the continued progress of Moore's law was extremely predictable since its inception in 1965 till more recently. When new drivers like *More-than-Moore* and *Beyond CMOS* are introduced to drive the growth of semiconductor business, there should be a well-defined goal that would define the progress that the overall industry needs to achieve in a specified time frame to drive the industrial growth. In this chapter, we will learn how to measure the progress of the semiconductor industry for years to come with new drivers like *More-than-Moore* and *Beyond CMOS*.

Macroeconomic Parameters for Measuring the Progress With *More-than-Moore* and *Beyond* CMOS

Let us start with the basics of supply and demand that drive the growth of an economy. As explained by Professor Ravi Batra in his article "Weapons of Mass Exploitation" published in truthout.org, for a healthy economy, supply must be equal to demand, or we have

$$Supply = Demand$$

However, when there is huge unemployment in the democratic society, this creates problems not only for the unemployed but also for elected officials, because the unemployed have the right to vote. Hence, career politicians seek to face a happy electorate and be re-elected. Due to government policies since the 1980s, the supply side economics has raised supply but has not let the real demand catch up with growing supply. Hence, if unemployment has been created as a result of poor economic demand, politicians are happy to create ways to let national spending rise to the level of supply so that supply would be equal to demand. As economist Ravi Batra says, career politicians face two choices, either follow policies that would raise salaries of Americans proportionately to the level of productivity—which is only fair and ethical—or to adopt measures to lure consumers into larger debt, so that consumers spend more not out of a pay raise, but from increased borrowing.

This process of luring the public into debt in order to get re-elected is political corruption. It is also corruption because these politicians, who are ever in need of campaign donations, do not want to offend the interests of their wealthy donors and crony capitalists, who do not wish to pay fair wages to their employees in proportion to labor productivity. The wages have been trailing productivity for several decades and elected officials have been following this kind of a monetary policy since 1981, which tempts people into larger debts. This eliminates unemployment as spending rises to the level of supply, because now,

$$Supply = Demand + New Consumer Debt$$

With this monetary policy, the Federal Reserve (Fed) prints more money to bring down the rate of interest and the lower interest rates (which has been 0 percent from 2006 until late 2015) induce people to increase their borrowing or their debt. However, the wage–productivity gap has been rising so fast that the government also has to raise its own spending and debt constantly so that total spending matches rising supply. In this case,

Supply = Demand + New Consumer Debt + New Government Debt

This "fiscal policy" raises the government's debt, but it just postpones the real problem of unemployment. This is how United States is awash in debt at both the consumer and the government level. The politicians follow such debt-creation policies to get re-elected, while creating an impression as if they are doing American workers a favor by preserving their jobs. Instead, they are simply enriching themselves and crony capitalists, without solving the real problem of unemployment which results from a growing gap between wages and productivity.

Now, let us observe how the progress of Moore's law can help in solving the problem of unemployment in global economy. In fact, global unemployment is precisely what is bringing the progress of Moore's law to a standstill due to poor return on investment (RoI). Just as an example, if we consider the number of transistors manufactured by Intel Inc. for every generation of the progress of Moore's law to contribute to "supply" into the economy and the consumer demand for them as contributor to "demand" for these transistors, then any unemployment would represent a loss of demand. Hence, we have

Number of Transistors (SUPPLY) = Real Wages (REAL DEMAND) + Consumer Debt + National Debt

The supply of transistors is well documented from the consistent progress of Moore's law. However, it is difficult to find the real wages which are not well documented but there is an evidence of wages being suppressed because of policies of globalization as explained in the chapter entitled "Globalization of Semiconductor Manufacturing" in my volume *Mass Capitalism* (2014). While the exact consumer debt is huge, which is evident from the fact that most Americans live paycheck-to-paycheck and have mortgaged their cars and houses, there is no exact quantitative measure of consumer debt on the national level. Hence, the only measuring

Table 8.1 A comparison of progress of Moore's law for Intel
processors from 1971 to 2012 with national debt per transistor

Year	Intel Processor Transistor Count[1]	Approx. U.S. National Debt[2]	National Debt/ Transistor
1971	2,300	398,129,744,455	652173913
1972	3,500	427,260,460,940	428571428.6
1974	4,500	475,059,815,731	333333333.3
1976	6,500	620,433,000,000	276923076.9
1978	29,000	771,544,000,000	65517241.4
1982	134,000	1,142,034,000,000	14925373.1
1985	275,000	1,823,103,000,000	10909090.9
1989	1,180,235	2,857,430,960,187	3389155.6
1993	3,100,000	4,411,488,883,139	1774193.5
1995	5,500,000	4,973,982,900,013	1090909.1
1997	7,500,000	5,413,146,011,397	866666.7
1999	9,500,000	5,656,270,901,615	684210.5
2000	21,000,000	5,674,178,209,886	300000
2001	45,000,000	5,807,463,412,200	151111.1
2002	55,000,000	6,228,235,965,597	127272.7
2004	112,000,000	7,379,052,696,330	66964.3
2005	169,000,000	7,932,709,661,723	46745.6
2006	184,000,000	8,506,973,899,215	44565.2
2007	411,000,000	9,007,653,372,262	20681.3
2008	731,000,000	10,024,724,896,912	12311.9
2010	1,170,000,000	13,561,623,030,891	10256.4
2012	1,400,000,000	16,066,241,407,385	9785.7

Source: 1Wikipedia-Transistor Count
          2www.treasurydirect.gov/govt/reports/pd/histdebt_histo5.htm

entity that correlates to the dropping real economic demand is the rising
national debt of America. Fortunately, there also exists a national debt
ceiling but even the debt ceiling has been raised several times by the politicians instead of solving the real cause of unemployment—the growing
gap between supply and demand. Today, this national debt is above U.S.
$19 trillion.

From Figure 8.3, we observe that the ratio of national debt per transistor is steadily decreasing exponentially in the economy which could be
considered as a deflationary impact of progress of Moore's law on national

U.S. National Debt (1971 -2012)

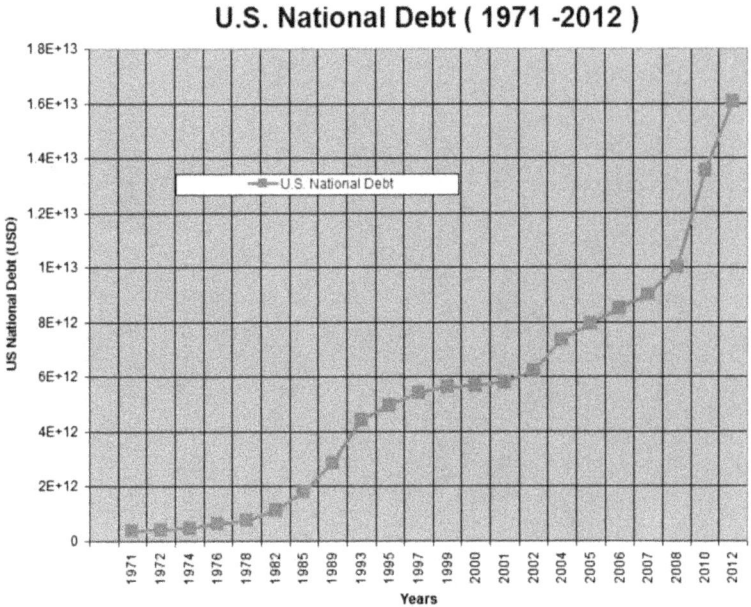

Figure 8.1 Approx. U.S. national debt increase from 1971 to 2012

Intel Processor Transistor Count (1971-2012)

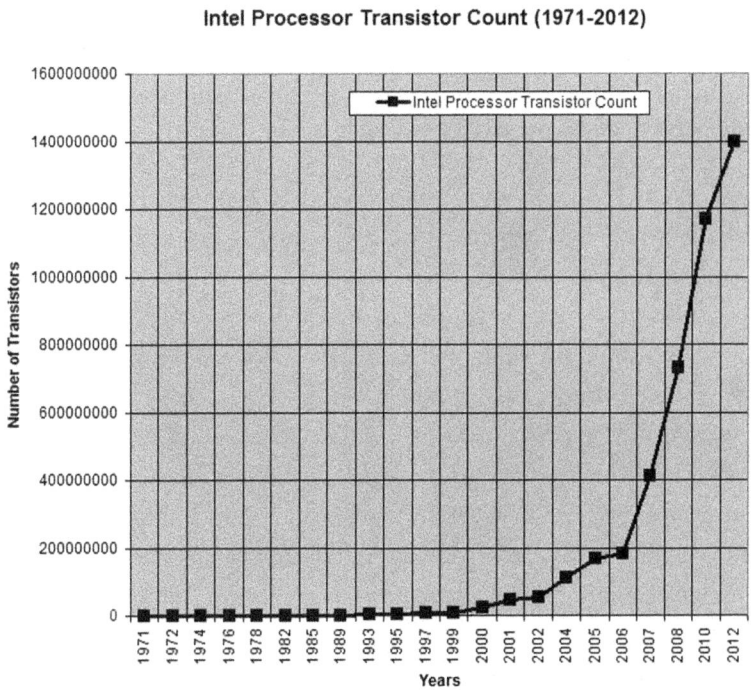

Figure 8.2 The increase in transistor count for Intel processors from 1971 to 2012

Deflationary impact of Moore's Law on U.S. National Debt

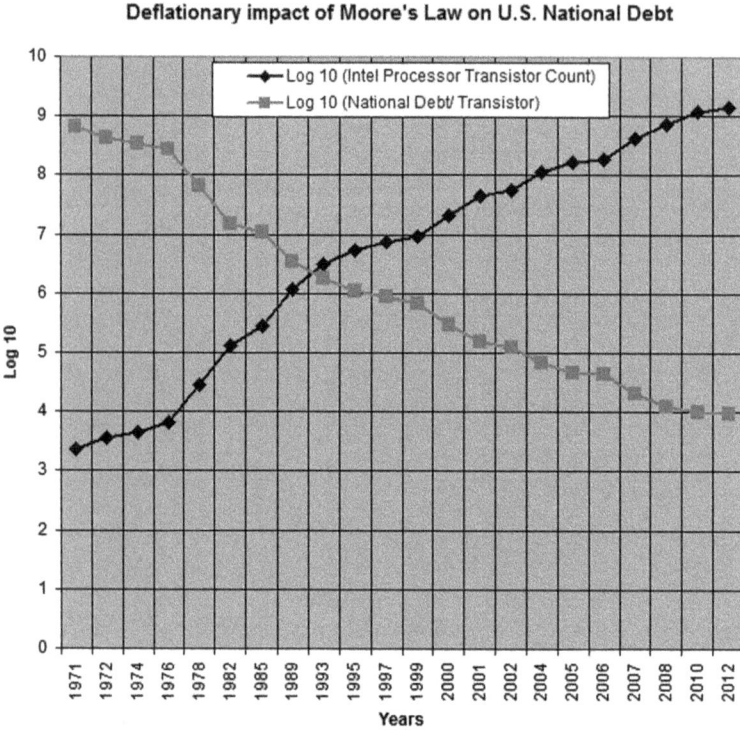

Figure 8.3 *The deflationary impact of the progress of Moore's law on U.S. national debt from 1971 to 2012*

debt. However, if you observe this trend, we notice that before 1991, this trend has been symmetrical, but since 1991 until 2012, we observe that the transistor count is continuing to grow but with United States reaching its national debt ceiling; this graph has ceased to show an exact symmetry when compared to the exponential growth trend for the transistor count. While the elected politicians in the Democratic Party, which is in power in the United States, want to raise the debt limit by trying to enrich themselves from their corporate donors, the Republican Party, which is in opposition, has proposed cutting the entitlement spending for the jobless Americans thereby worsening poverty in the United States. Neither of these political parties shows any intention to restore a free market economy where the wages of Americans would catch up with their productivity, but instead both parties wish to continue the policies that favor their wealthy campaign financiers. These policies are steadily decreasing the consumer purchasing power, increasing poverty in United States as well as are raising U.S. national debt to reach its debt limit. Hence, Moore's law is now slowing down and it is believed by the semiconductor industry that it would be the economics of manufacturing that would lead to the demise of Moore's law.

However, as explained previously, this national debt is the only measurable entity of the net loss in real economic demand at national level due to the falling real wages of the domestic workforce. If national debt is allowed to grow exponentially forever, then the progress of Moore's law, which is based on supply-side economics, can continue forever. But, no country can have an infinite limit on its credit card and what has been borrowed will have to be repaid. Additionally, as explained before, this exponential growth in U.S. national debt has been caused by increased government spending by delaying the real problem of unemployment caused by the growing gap between real wages and productivity of the workforce, which causes a gap between real demand from low wages and actual demand required to sustain the supply of transistors manufactured into the economy. Hence, the only way to sustain the progress of Moore's law and to continue benefiting from its innovations is to raise the economic demand to catch up with the rising productivity resulting from exponential growth in supply of transistors in the economy with the continued progress of Moore's law.

Today the U.S. national debt is above $19 trillion. Therefore, the total loss in real wages since 1971 has been approximately above $19 trillion. (Here, we have included the student loan debts as part of the equation. The student loan debts have resulted from skyrocketing costs of higher education and borrowers being unable to service their debts in a timely fashion because of lack of sufficient well-paying jobs after graduation, which further reduces their real wages when the interests on their student loan debts rise.) In addition to reducing student loan debt, if consumer debt could also be minimized through free market economic reforms, we would have a much higher demand to absorb the increased supply of transistors in the economy, which would ensure a sustainable consumption of manufactured electronics and sustain an increased demand for more electronics. In this way, the progress of Moore's law could continue until physical limitations play a role in arresting the progress of this law.

In this situation, *More-than-Moore* and *Beyond CMOS* could serve as drivers for sustaining the continued investments toward boosting the processing power of transistors. However, based on the graph in Figure 8.3, it can be concluded that any amount of new transistors that would be manufactured would not get consumed as U.S. national debt cannot grow forever. As "monetary policy" does not let wages keep pace with productivity, the real demand will never be able to sustain the consumption of transistors manufactured with the continued progress of Moore's law. This is precisely why there is a poor economic demand for foundries manufacturing 10-nm transistors. This would put any plans for *More-than-Moore* and *Beyond CMOS* to arrive at a standstill. Hence, in order to sustain the progress of *More-than-Moore* and *Beyond CMOS*, I propose a complete shift from supply-side economics and advocate the demand-side economic drivers like the "minimum necessities" and "maximum amenities" as will be elaborated in the following chapter.

Conclusion

The 50 years of progress of Moore's law has also been accompanied by a transformation of U.S. economy and its semiconductor industry. The U.S. economy has transformed from a free market enterprise to "crony capitalism." The progress of Moore's law for more than 30 years has been based on supply-side economics. This has resulted in an unsustainable consumer debt and national debt by shrinking the real consumer demand in the economy. The demand has continued to grow by means of raising the consumer and national debt and not by letting the real wages of consumers grow in proportion to their rising productivity. Hence, in order that *More-than-Moore* and *Beyond CMOS* are able to drive the growth of the U.S. and global semiconductor industry, ITRS and the semiconductor industry has to adopt the demand-side economic drivers instead of supply-side economic drivers. When the demand-side economic drivers are able to continuously raise the consumer purchasing power in the economy, it would act as an incentive for raising the economic demand in a sustainable way and gradually eliminate the consumer and national debt in the U.S. and global economy.

Suggested Readings

[1] Mulay, Apek, *Mass Capitalism: A Blueprint for Economic Revival*, Book Publishers Network, Bothell, WA, 2014.

[2] Mulay, Apek, *Sustaining Moore's Law: Uncertainty Leading to a Certainty of IoT Revolution*, Morgan & Claypool Publishers, San Rafael, CA, 2015.

[3] Batra, Ravi, "*Weapons of Mass Exploitation*", Truthout.org. May 8, 2011. http://www.truth-out.org/news/item/952:weapons-of-mass-exploitation

[4] Treasury Direct, "*Government - Historical Debt Outstanding - Annual (1950-1999, 2000-2015)*". www.treasurydirect.gov/govt/reports/pd/histdebt_histo5.htm

[5] Wikipedia. "Transistor Count". https://en.wikipedia.org/wiki/Transistor_count

[6] Sarkar, Prabhat Ranjan, *PROUT in a Nutshell*, Ananda Marga Publications, Kolkata, India, 1959.

CHAPTER 9

Mass Capitalism's Minimum Necessities and Maximum Amenities for Driving Growth of *More-than-Moore* and *Beyond* CMOS

Introduction

As we have learned from the previous chapters, the progress of Moore's law in the U.S. semiconductor industry has been driven by supply-side economic policies. As a result of focusing only on the supply of silicon and no focus on the growth in the real economic demand, the progress of Moore's law has been made possible by growth of consumer debt and national debt. This has taken the U.S. economy and its semiconductor industry on a path of unsustainable growth. Hence, for the semiconductor industry to progress with *More-than-Moore* and *Beyond CMOS, a* robust growth of economic demand is critical. This growth in economic demand should be sustainable. While driving the economic growth, it has to be noted that both consumer debt and national debt have to be gradually reduced but the progress of Moore's law has to continue to drive more innovations and improve the technological productivity. In that regard, I propose the following demand-side economic drivers for sustaining the progress of *More-than-Moore* and *Beyond CMOS*.

"Minimum Necessities" and "Maximum Amenities"

How to further drive the growth in economic demand so that the economic progress with *More-than-Moore* and *Beyond CMOS* can be sustained? Free market economic reforms would enable the supply of transistors, from a continuous progress of Moore's law, to grow in proportion to their demand. When supply equals demand, any further increase in the supply of transistors from the progress of Moore's law would need a proportional increase in their demand. To keep this progress sustainable, instead of increasing the consumer and national debt, a better approach is to shift the macroeconomic policy from supply-side economics to demand-side economics, which could be driven by growth in real wages through "minimum necessities" and "maximum amenities," which would be discussed in detail in this chapter.

In my volume *Sustaining Moore's Law*(2015), I made a case that the progress of Moore's law has essentially been a progress of supply-side economics. The progress of Moore's law has focused only on the supply of transistors and the real economic demand has been completely ignored for more than 30 years. Hence, when free market reforms meet a roadblock, any further progress of *More-than-Moore* and *Beyond CMOS* is only possible as long as the consumer demand keeps rising in the economy to sustain the consumption of exponentially rising supply of transistors in consumer electronics. Hence, we need an innovative approach for ensuring a growth in economic demand to further drive the supply of consumer electronics into the economy without an increase in consumer and national debt.

I had also briefly mentioned about the terms "minimum necessities" and "maximum amenities" in the chapter entitled "From an Unsustainable to a Sustainable Progress of Moore's Law" in my volume *Sustaining Moore's Law*(2015). We need to implement economic solutions for sustaining the progress of Moore's law through the establishment of a true free market economy where the real job creators in the economy are not only the producers but also the consumers. Without a healthy consumer demand for the latest and greatest electronic products, any further investments toward the progress of Moore's law, transition to 450-mm silicon wafers, EUV lithography improvements, *More-than-Moore* as well as *Beyond CMOS* are bound to provide a poor return on investments (RoI) for the producers of electronic goods.

Every human being in this world has certain minimum necessities like food, clothing, shelter, and education to lead a life of dignity. The minimum necessities of human society should be met through a growth in consumer purchasing power in the economy. Semiconductor industry professionals are not only to recognize the importance of higher consumer purchasing power in the economy but should also be actively involved in ushering in true free market economic reforms that guarantee the growth in consumer purchasing power in the economy for the continued progress of Moore's law. It also becomes a social responsibility to provide individuals with a higher purchasing power. When such free market reforms based on *mass capitalism* are carried out, there would be special incentives provided to individuals with special abilities. Each and every human being requires clothes, medicine, housing accommodation, proper education, food for proper nourishment, etc. These demands must be fulfilled by means of providing work by creating jobs and not by means of offering any kind of doles.

While free markets ensure that wages catch up with productivity, there should be special amenities provided to intellectuals, scientists, and people performing special services. However, when offering these amenities, it needs to be ensured that the consumer purchasing power of the overall economy also grows while minimizing the chances of the growth of large disparities in the economy. There will always be a gap between the minimum necessities that decide the standard of living and special amenities that are offered to meritorious people. A free market approach to minimize the gap between minimum necessities and maximum amenities is to raise the consumer purchasing power through a productive use of technology, which would also boost the minimum necessities for all as well as raise the maximum amenities for meritorious people. For example, in a certain country, business leaders and intellectuals would require a luxury car, and these should be offered to them because of their profound contribution to the society. But after that endeavor, the buying power of other individuals should also proportionally increase so that they are able to afford to buy at least a motor bike, if not a car.

However, in this process of improving the consumer purchasing power by means of a productive use of technology, it could be noticed that after sometime, the purchasing power of business leaders and intellectuals need to be higher for them to be able to afford an airplane. In that regard the consumer purchasing power of the rest of economy (excluding the leaders and intellectuals) should also be high enough (to keep economic disparity in check) so that they are be able to afford at least an ordinary car, if not a luxury one. This progressive increase in the standard of living should be carried out with a minimal of government intervention because in true free markets the role of government is small and its intervention into the economy is minimal. Diversity is the law of nature and it is impossible to do away with diversity. However, if this approach of raising the standard of living of society is adopted, then it would be possible to raise the standard of living for all citizens in an economy while still rewarding hard work and merit.

As a matter of fact, the above-mentioned approach would be a sustainable one as it would ensure that the consumer debt and national debt do not grow, so that the growth in consumer purchasing power of the overall economy is sustained. Although the gap between minimum necessities deciding the standard of living of citizens and the maximum amenities that are provided to meritorious people will remain unbridged forever, this gap between the two should not exceed certain limits; the gap exceeding limits resulted in recessions and depressions in the past for global economy. In this way, a productive use of technology would increase the consumer purchasing power such that wages would keep pace with the productivity of the workforce, thereby sustaining the progress of *More-than-Moore* and *Beyond CMOS* through a continued growth in consumer purchasing power. One example of the productive use of technology over an unproductive use of the same can be given, which is based on the unemployment created in today's economy because of the use of automation.

Today, many modern economic thinkers blame automation, based on technological progress, as a major cause of job losses. However, technology could be productively utilized in such a way that the manufacturing sector could cut back on work hours while paying workers a high wage due to their high productivity resulting from the use of technology. This is because automation enables a worker to be highly productive through the use of machines in order to manufacture products. High worker productivity significantly increases the supply of goods into the economy. As a result of this increased productivity from the progress of technology, workers would need to work for fewer number of hours to achieve their production target. They could use their spare time to pursue higher education, leisure, hobbies, vocational training, etc. In this way, it is also possible to minimize, if not eliminate, the problem of high unemployment resulting from automation while still keeping the supply of goods proportionate to consumer demand, thereby maintaining an economic balance.

Now that we have explained the "minimum necessities" and "maximum amenities," let us also discuss a practical way to envision this approach. In any economic system, the workers are producers on one side as they contribute to the supply of goods into the economy by being productive at their jobs but on the other hand they also contribute to the economic demand when they spend their wages. Hence, every human being has a great economic contribution by means of sustaining the economic demand. Over the last 30 years, supply-side economic policies have resulted in excess supply but have led to a poor economic demand. This rising supply has been balanced by rising consumer debt and national debt; making it highly unsustainable.

If the supply-side economic policies that have been driving the progress of Moore's law are replaced by demand-side economic policies, then there would be a focus on growth driven by the economic demand in an economy. As the economic demand grows, new businesses would be created that would cater to this demand. In this way, there would be a multiplying effect in the economy where demand drives more supply and that supply in turn drives more demand which would engender a new virtuous cycle of semiconductor industry. Besides, such an approach would also put a halt to the creation of consumer debt making the resulting progress sustainable. Free market economic reforms based on the theory of *mass capitalism* would ensure that trade and budget deficits are eliminated. In this way, the growth in economic demand due to demand-side economic policies would result in a sustainable economic growth as compared to the growth in supply with supply-side economic policies.

Now let us observe how to implement these demand-side economic drivers for *More-than-Moore* and *Beyond CMOS* approach. I would like to demonstrate the importance of employee stock options (ESOPs) for a neo-cooperative corporation as a way to guide how the demand-side economic drivers are to be adjusted to ensure that there is a fair share for one's hard work. Suppose there is a publicly traded neo-cooperative corporation with 100 employees having 1,000 publicly traded shares in total. As per the theory of *mass capitalism*, at least 51 percent of these 1,000 shares should in the hands of company employees. Hence, only 490 shares can be offered for purchase by any nonemployee investor of such a company. Since, majority shares are retained by the employees, all key decisions are in the hands of company employees and nonemployee investors are not able to dictate the company's internal working and policies. Since employees are majority shareholders, the CEO and board of directors shall be directly appointed by employees.

The employees, who purchase shares in the neo-cooperative corporation, should have no power or right to transfer their shares without the permission of the other shareholders, but their shares may be inherited. If these employees have no descendants, then their shares should pass on to their legally authorized successors who could become shareholders if they are not already shareholders of the corporation. The reason for this policy is that it prevents a few cronies from purchasing large numbers of shares of a corporation and speculating in the market place. This type of economic activity is precisely one of the causes of ongoing economic depression. Besides, by ownership of company shares, the employees would also become part-owners and hence more responsible.

Of the total of 510 shares, majority of the shares would be given to employees based on their productive contributions toward the growth of the company. However, a few shares would be retained to reward top performing employees and give them a chance to rise higher in the organization. Let us say, 100 shares are retained for top performing employees and rest 410 shares are distributed among 100 employees in proportion to their productive contribution which means that, a person who is more experienced and contributes more toward the growth of the company deserves more shares than other contributors. The "minimum necessity" would guarantee that all employees would have a stake in the success of the business. This does not limit it only to the C-suite employees but will be offered to employees at the lowest section of corporate ladder, like the janitor of the organization. In this way, even the janitor will work hard and make sacrifices when needed toward the growth of the organization because she or he has a stake in the success of the organization by being a part-owner. The organization shall have different departments, and hence, the organization's role will be more decentralized.

The managerial responsibilities shall be shared by employees and this would reduce the workload on managers as well as reduce the need of highly paid "project managers," thereby shouldering a more pay with higher responsibilities to several employees. This has two advantages, viz. every employee would become more responsible and accountable toward the success of the business. Besides, it will reduce the load on managers and provide an extra pay for more responsibilities to company employees, thereby providing a fairness or transparency in employee performance reviews because there would be fairness in the recognition of hardworking or high-achieving employees, and this would not depend on any personal likes or dislikes of a single supervisor. The shares for top performing individuals will be allocated every quarter or annually based on the operating profits of the organization.

The "maximum amenity" would also play an important role in gauging the performance reviews in an organization. Certain employees are much better than their peers and if the organization policies do not offer growth for other employees who are equally hardworking but not as talented as the top performers, it would result in poor job satisfaction. In order to retain the top performers as well as several other hardworking employees, when assigning the 100 shares for top performers, it will also be ensured that rewarding of shares will be limited to its maximum value to any employee. For example, a top performer could get a maximum of 3 shares out of 100. This would leave sufficient number of shares to reward other performers and thereby retain all the employees in the organization alongwith rewarding the top performers. When the hard work results in increase in share price of the company, it will indirectly benefit not only individual employees by means of raising their purchasing power but would also benefit the nonemployee investors by providing them a good RoI.

Semiconductor industry leaders need to realize that the present roadblocks for transition to 450-mm diameter silicon wafers by the industry have resulted from the stoppage in the rolling of money in the economy. The industry leaders also need to realize that the number of consumable commodities in the world is limited, but all human beings need their basic necessities for survival. If one person accumulates too much wealth and instead of investing just hoards his or her wealth, this will generally mean that others will be deprived of even their minimum necessities in life. This is precisely what has resulted in a poor economic demand and bringing the profitability from mass production of 450-mm diameter silicon wafers to a standstill. A failure to recognize the fact that economic demand depends on being able to satisfy the needs of others is itself a psychic disease. But the victims of this ailment are all human beings when an economic depression hits the economy suffering from a poor economic demand.

However, a huge unemployment can be avoided by means of formulating neo-cooperative corporations. In these forms of organizations, whenever there are economic downturns, the employees will take across-the-board pay cuts as all employees are shareholders or joint owners of the company. Hence, there would be a consensus on such decisions as every employee will be able to voice his or her opinion as a shareholder of the company. Also, the nonemployee investors will not be able to force the company to cut down the work force in order for them to get a higher RoI in an economic downturn like it happens in today's crony capitalism. As a company grows, more stock options would be available, which would be offered to company employees such that a minimum of 51 percent of company shares are with the employees of the company. When it comes to a capital-intensive business like the semiconductor manufacturing industry, where huge capital allocation would be required, it would be possible to partner with the local government to keep those investments sustainable. The government will also earn a good RoI when there is more employment created in the economy. The three-tier business model for semiconductor industry envisions this approach to have government backing without government intervention in the economy.

In this way, "minimum necessities" would enable the good purchasing power to grow through hard work without using doles. In addition, "maximum amenities" would ensure a rational distribution of rewards to the top performers based on a consensus with minimal government intervention in the economy. When such an adjustment is maintained, hard work and merit would be rewarded and there will be no huge disparities in the economy. The minimum necessities vary from country to country and from region to region. Hence, an economic decentralization would ensure fairness in the distribution of all potentialities at the local level.

The "minimum necessities" of human society should be guaranteed only by creating more employment opportunities. The semiconductor industry professionals have to not only recognize the importance of these necessities to generate an economic demand for semiconductor products, but also consider it to be a social responsibility to guarantee the availability of good purchasing power to meet those necessities. It is not enough to provide the minimum necessities of life—simultaneously, the wealth of the country should also be increased. If sufficient wealth is not generated to meet the growing demands of the people, seeds of discontent will settle in their minds. Hence, whether or not there is a growth of population, there should also be an increase in national wealth. The growth in productivity from technological progress through *More-than-Moore* and *Beyond CMOS* drivers would play an important role in increasing the gross national wealth of a nation and "minimum necessities" and "maximum amenities" would help achieve that goal.

Every country that is planning to have a large and viable semiconductor industry in its economy should bear in mind that the "minimum necessities" will go on increasing day by day. If my proposed approach is adopted to sustain the progress of semiconductor industry through a growth in consumer purchasing power, in the not-too-distant future a day will arrive when every individual will be able to acquire sufficient purchasing power to be able to purchase not just a smartphone but much more powerful electronic gadgets to improve the overall productivity of the entire economy. This vision can be fulfilled only by means of creating sufficient purchasing capacity through a productive use of technology. However, it should be noted that if the "minimum necessities" are guaranteed without demanding any personal skill or labor, the individual may develop the psychology of idleness. This would hamper not only the progress of that individual and the overall economy but would also hamper the progress of *More-than-Moore* and *Beyond CMOS*.

Conclusion

The free market economic reforms needed for sustaining *More-than-Moore* and *Beyond CMOS* should be such that minimum necessities are met for a particular age and maximum amenities are to be offered to those with special abilities according to the degree of their merit. However, under all circumstances, there is an equal opportunity for access of maximum amenities for the common people. It should be noted that the minimum necessities of the age (as per their money value) and maximum amenities of the age (as per their money value) need to progressively keep adjusting. In this way, it would become possible to raise the standard of living for the overall economy. It would enable economic growth to continue forever in a free market economy without resulting in any economic recessions and depressions.

Suggested Readings

[1] Mulay, Apek, *Mass Capitalism: A Blueprint for Economic Revival*, Book Publishers Network, Bothell, WA, 2014.
[2] Mulay, Apek, *Sustaining Moore's Law: Uncertainty Leading to a Certainty of IoT Revolution*, Morgan & Claypool Publishers, San Rafael,CA, 2015.
[3] Sarkar, Prabhat Ranjan, *PROUT in a Nutshell*, Ananda Marga Publications, Kolkata, India, 1959.

CHAPTER 10

Increasing Broader Economic Prosperity by Driving Economic Demand of Consumer Electronics with Progress of *More-than-Moore* and *Beyond CMOS*

Introduction

The existence of any kind of exploitation in an economy could be ascertained through the prevalence of such factors as extreme poverty, social insecurity, social injustices against the common people, lack of purchasing power to acquire the minimum requirements of life, huge economic and social differences between various classes, the irrational distribution of wealth, etc. The present social, economic, and political conditions in several countries across the world having democratic governments including the world's most prosperous representative republic, the United States, as well as the world's most populous democracy, India, exemplify all these ailments. Hence, both countries seem to be on the verge of social revolution because of a complete failure of the career politicians in being able to address national macroeconomic problems. In that regard, it becomes necessary to address the causes of poverty and offer some practical free market economic solutions toward raising global prosperity through a continued industrial and economic growth.

Economic Exploitation and Demise of Moore's Law

Today, we are living in a most unusual global economy. Political corruption in major democracies is now becoming more and more painfully evident all over the world; the over-accumulation of wealth by a small segment of population and the resulting poverty for the majority is upsetting the global economic balance. Today, along with the wealthy nations, even the developing economies are beginning to realize the importance of having a smaller size of government to minimize the political corruption. At this crucial moment in world history, proper leadership is essential to revive the industry and economy. But, even more essential is to have a logical and free market approach toward raising global prosperity.

There are various types of exploitation in a society. The form and character of this exploitation could change as per changes in time, place, and person. In the economic sphere, exploitation has taken the forms of feudal exploitation, colonial exploitation, capitalist exploitation, imperialist exploitation, and fascist exploitation. Exploitation may also manifest in such spheres as the physical, psychic, economic, political, and cultural spheres. In the past, the slave system was very much prevalent in the Greek and Roman empires, where the rulers exploited the vanquished to bolster their own interests.

In economic exploitation, the vested interests deprive ordinary people of their minimum requirements. Money lending, charging exorbitant interest rates, compelling the small businesses to sell their produce through distress sales, etc. are examples of economic exploitation. The 2008 financial crisis in the U.S. economy started because of the major bankruptcies that have resulted out of an intention to profit from the exploitation of low-income Americans. It was well known to the big banks that they would be bailed out and the tax payers will have to pay for their bailout. While millions of American citizens were thrown out to streets, the bankers became richer through profiteering from such exploitation which has plunged the U.S. and global economy into an ongoing economic stagnation. Regardless of the type of exploitation carried out by the exploiters, when exploitation becomes excessive, the society starts moving toward revolution. In this process, the role of the exploiters gets exposed as they fail to disguise their exploitation any longer.

Due to the defective mentality, such as "Let others live in destitution, but I want immense wealth; let others be landless, but I want landed property," many people have suffered in the past, and many are still suffering today. This results in the start of violence and exploitation and eventually ends with violence and exploitation. Thus, it has been rightly said, "violence begets violence." History has demonstrated that if a person becomes a billionaire by exploiting the masses, the same exploited masses, driven to irrepressible violence by poverty and hunger, will snatch away that billionaire's accumulated wealth and raze his honor to the ground. It is common sense to understand that every limited resource of the world should be rationally utilized for the greater benefit of the majority. However, if a few individuals amass all the limited amount of wealth then it kills the consumer demand in the economy and drags the global economy into a depression. The decreasing consumer demand has not only reduced the return on investments (RoI) for transitioning to 450-mm diameter silicon wafers for global semiconductor industry but it has also drastically reduced the ability of Moore's law to drive economic growth. Hence, we need a better economic system where there is a rational distribution of available limited economic resources such that people get a fair share for their hard work, without any intervention of the government, and the system does not lead to any form of exploitation.

History is awash with examples of the rise of Robin Hoods, who considered it to be a virtuous deed to plunder the wealth of the wealthy individuals and distribute it among those in need. The Robin Hoods of the medieval period perhaps thought that this was the best way to eradicate social disparity. However, this has never worked in the long run and this approach would not work in creating global prosperity. In nearly every country of the world such Robin Hoods are emerging today through democratic elections, but just as the Robin Hoods have not been able to solve the problem of social inequality in the past, modern Robin Hoods would not be able to solve these problems by means of plundering the wealth. The modern Robin Hoods call on having a bigger size of government by means of sharply raising the taxes on the richest and giving doles to the poor with that money. Not only does this process suppress hard work but it also reduces an incentive toward economic progress through innovations and other creative contributions. The main reason of the failure of this process is that no economic system can survive on charity for a long time. Such an approach only creates a society of beggars. This type of a greedy, indolent, and inactive society foretells even greater poverty in the future. Moreover, plundering the wealth of the wealthy does not eliminate the root causes of economic exploitation, because although robbery may reduce the assets of the wealthy, it does not destroy the seed of exploitation. Besides, it creates an attitude of revenge in the minds of the wealthy individuals and corporations, which eventually causes more exploitation in society.

A Free Market Solution to Raise Global Prosperity—A Rapid Progress of the Global Semiconductor Industry With *More-than-Moore* and *Beyond* CMOS

A vibrant domestic semiconductor eco-system is critical to sustain the progress of today's knowledge-based economy. It is also equally important for a robust semiconductor ecosystem to usher in the fourth industrial revolution in the form of Internet of things (*IoT*). I believe that the free market economic approach that I have presented in this volume to sustain the progress of *More-than-Moore* and *Beyond CMOS* in global semiconductor industry would play an essential role in raising broader prosperity in the global economy through a rapid growth of consumer purchasing power with a productive use of semiconductor technology.

The progress of global semiconductor industry through the use of advanced scientific technology achieved with the progress of Moore's law would mean rapid automation in every sector of the economy. The ones who are conservative could vociferously criticize this automation. Actually, such automation, when implemented in an unbalanced economic system, inevitably brings more misery, in the form of unemployment to the masses. That is why conservative people will oppose it. This is one of the reasons why in an unbalanced economic system, where citizens want to promote public good without antagonizing the owners of capital, these citizens will be left with no other choice but to oppose automation. This is because when the productive capacity of machinery is doubled, the required human labor is decreased by half, so it would need retrenchment of a large numbers of workers from their factories. But, if automation is opposed, the progress of the semiconductor industry will also come to a standstill.

However, a few optimists may say, "Under circumstantial pressure other ways will be found to employ these surplus laborers in different jobs, and the very effort to find these alternatives will accelerate scientific advancement, so the ultimate result of automation, is in fact, good." This view, though not useless, has no practical value in any unbalanced economy, because it is not possible to arrange new jobs for retrenched workers as quickly as they become surplus laborers due to rapid automation. As a matter of fact, in today's unbalanced global economy, surplus laborers get ruined, bit by bit, due to poverty and hunger. A few among them are trying to keep body and soul together by depending on unemployment benefits provided by government. When these benefits expire and they are still unable to find any employment, they would resort to petty theft, armed robbery, violence, and other sorts of antisocial activities. This situation is certainly not desirable in an economy. The reduced consumer purchasing power also indirectly hurts the technological progress. However, modern technological advances and scientific progress has to continue benefiting today's knowledge-based economy. The only way to achieve a balance between the two is to have macroeconomic reforms in the economy based on the free market economic theory of *mass capitalism*, which shall ensure a growth in both supply and demand by ensuring that wages keep pace with productivity.

It should be noted that a huge unemployment caused by technological growth is unsustainable for overall macroeconomic growth. This is because future technological growth depends on the investment of huge capital. However, if there is huge unemployment in an economy and loss in consumer purchasing power, then there would be a poor RoI due to a lack of economic demand. This is precisely why the RoI is so low in the semiconductor industry at a technology node of 10-nm transistor gate length. However, in *mass capitalism*-based free market economic system, there is no scope for such an unhealthy situation to occur because the balance between supply and demand will always be maintained. In *mass capitalism*, automation will lead to less labor hours depending on the output but would provide a higher prosperity. With the doubling of the productivity of machines, the working hours of laborers will be reduced by half in order to reduce the gap between wages and productivity, which would in turn reduce the gap between supply and demand.

Of course, this reduction in working hours will have to be determined keeping in view the demand for commodities and the availability of labor to meet that desired output. In this way, a productive use of technology would benefit the progress of entire human race. It is also possible that as a result of automation, the semiconductor industry could completely automate the production of semiconductor chips from the beginning to the end which is often referred to as "lights-out fab." It would also be possible that in a not-too-distant future, people will have sufficient purchasing power so that no one will be required to work for more than a few hours a week to meet all their essential necessities resulting from a continuous technological progress of *More-than-Moore* and *Beyond CMOS*. Not always being preoccupied with the problems of acquiring food, clothing, etc., people's creativity and other subtle potentialities will no longer be wasted. They will be able to devote ample time to such activities as sports, literary pursuits as well as subtle spiritual practices such as meditation, which have proven to improve the creativity of employees and increase their personal satisfaction and fulfillment.

Mass Capitalism Makes it Feasible to Have a Happy Blending of Rationality and Creativity as Semiconductor Industry Advances With More-than-Moore and Beyond CMOS Economic Drivers

As the global semiconductor industry progresses on the path of *More-than-Moore* and *Beyond CMOS*, there is a necessity of having a free market economic system, which offers a fair opportunity to procure certain minimum requirements by ensuring that wages of the workforce in the economy catch up with the productivity of the workforce. However, the free market economic system should also provide *maximum amenities* to meritorious people. These two approaches would help sustain the economic demand and drive the growth of the semiconductor industry by meeting the minimum necessities of human society in order to generate an increasing economic demand for the latest and greatest electronic gadgets.

The minimum requirements must go on increasing according to the physical needs of human beings and according to the changes in climatic conditions, environment, etc. Unless minimum requirements are satisfied, it would be difficult for human beings to drive economic demand for consumer electronics as majority of the consumer electronics are as of today "amenities" rather than "necessities" for the majority of population in developing and underdeveloped economies. Thus, the range of minimum requirements should also go on increasing according to the range of human social conditions. For example, the minimum necessities of citizens in the United States are much different from the minimum necessities of citizens of poor African countries. However, for both populations it is equally important to drive the economic demand in order to drive the progress of *More-than-Moore* and *Beyond CMOS*. There should also be fair chance for maximum amenities to be achievable for one and all. These amenities should be permitted to increase for the entire social order by having a true free market economy. In addition, this approach has to be practical and not an un-psychological one.

Suppose there is a bright lamp. Hundreds and thousands of insects would rush toward it and get burnt. Similarly, communism was like a bright lamp. Marxists built castles in the air. They preached high ideals and proposed principles that they claimed would transform the world, but they never thought about the practical application of their socioeconomic approach. They killed many innocent people and sent countless others to concentration camps in the name of so-called communist ideology. Stalin killed hundreds of thousands of people instead of helping them with amenities. In the name of doing good for the masses, Stalin had killed so many people. This was thoroughly against humanism. Today, most countries in the world have rejected the rotten philosophy of communism.

If the common people and the meritorious people are treated as the same, the capable people will not receive the encouragement to develop their higher potentiality. This is the reason why brain drain has happened in the past in many developing economies such as India. The talented people who left India have perhaps left for good and would never come back unless they feel India can provide them the same amenities that have been offered to them in developed economies. Providing special amenities for those with special capabilities will stop future brain drain in India, and this way local talent can be preserved. These talented individuals can make great economic contributions to their domestic economies and help drive the progress of their domestic semiconductor industry. However, while implementing this it needs to be ensured that the economic disparity is always kept in check because huge disparities have resulted in recessions and depressions in the past and is also the root cause of ongoing economic stagnation in the global economy.

Acceleration is the spirit of technological progress, the spirit of economic progress as well as the spirit of the existential faculty of all human beings. One may not be a genius, that is one may simply be a member of the ordinary public, but even then the economic planning should allow such ordinary people to procure the minimum requirements for living a healthy life and provide them an incentive toward achieving the maximum amenities, which are made available in an ever-increasing manner according to the environmental conditions concerned and according to the demands of the day. Only when there is a rational allocation of resources and productive utilization of technology, can economic demand continue to drive the progress of semiconductor industry with a continued progress of *More-than-Moore* and *Beyond CMOS*. Only under such circumstances would it become possible to have a balanced economy that provides ample free time for individuals to devote time towards subtle pursuits that enhances human creativity.

The importance of human creativity can be understood from the success achieved by the Silicon Valley legend Steve Jobs. In an article entitled "How a Calligraphy Pen Rewrote Steve Jobs' Life," the author claims that calligraphing like a monk gave Steve Jobs an esthetic sense most math-nerd tech giants (like Bill Gates) lack. In his own words, Steve Jobs had said,

> I learned about serif and sans serif typefaces, about varying the amount of space between different letter combinations, about what makes great typography great. It was beautiful, historical, artistically subtle in a way that science can't capture.

This scope of improving human creativity can be expanded to a much larger percentage of human population only when there is a productive utilization of technology, which provides an ample free time to all participants in order to pursue their creative pursuits that would drive the growth of global semiconductor industry. *Mass capitalism*-based balanced economy could help to achieve that goal by means of meeting the minimum necessities of the workforce and offering maximum amenities to the workforce in extracting their creative contributions. Only under such conditions can there be a happy blending of rationality and creativity in an economy.

Conclusion

As the semiconductor industry advances with ideas based on the free market economic theory of *mass capitalism*, the progress of Moore's law will drive more investments into the economy. These proposed economic reforms would result in an economic solidarity, an increase in trade and commerce, more investment, more employment, and an improvement in the position of industry alongwith the overall economy. The rising productivity from the technological progress would result in the growth of the overall standard of living when wages of employees will keep pace with their productivity. The businesses would wholeheartedly embrace automation and supply chains would ensure an enhanced cooperation between different entities acting in the best interest of the supply chain. These reforms in developed economies are sure to be emulated by countries around the world, thereby leading to a better global macroeconomic growth, along with growth of local economies. In addition, these reforms would also help bring about global prosperity and usher in a vibrant growth of domestic and national economy by means of establishing a true free market and a balanced economy. Without *mass capitalism* based balanced and free market economic reforms, any further progress of semiconductor industry would further the problem of unemployment in domestic economy making any future progress unsustainable.

Suggested Readings

[1] Mulay, Apek, *Mass Capitalism: A Blueprint for Economic Revival*, Book Publishers Network, Bothell, WA, 2014.
[2] Mulay, Apek, *Sustaining Moore's Law: Uncertainty Leading to a Certainty of IoT Revolution*, Morgan & Claypool Publishers, San Rafael, CA, 2015.

[3] Sarkar, Prabhat Ranjan, *PROUT in a Nutshell*, Ananda Marga Publications, Kolkata, India, 1959.

[4] Mulay, Apek, *"Can an Economic System Make It Feasible to Have a Happy Blending of Rationality and Spirituality?"*, LinkedIn. September 3, 2015. https://www.linkedin.com/pulse/can-economic-system-make-feasible-have -happy-blending-mulay-apek-?trk=mp-reader-card

[5] Appelo, Tim, *"How a Calligraphy Pen Rewrote Steve Jobs' Life"*, The Hollywood Reporter, October 14, 2011. http://www.hollywoodreporter.com/news/steve -jobs-death-apple-calligraphy-248900

CHAPTER 11

Mass Capitalism and Fourth Industrial Revolution with More-than-Moore and Beyond CMOS

Introduction

The upcoming fourth industrial revolution in the form of "Internet of things" (IoT) is likely to offer a huge market that would allow low-cost chips and sensors to be attached to everyday consumer electronics such as refrigerators, washing machines, television, etc. It would also make it possible for refrigerator to order food or washing machines to ask clothes for laundering instructions, etc. It would be possible for local government to monitor traffic, pollution, and to offer a host of diverse services to their citizens. In this chapter, we will look into how the progress of *More-than-Moore* and *Beyond CMOS* along with the drivers proposed by the ITRS shall establish a new golden age of high prosperity and growth in the global semiconductor industry. The benefits of this growth would also radiate far and wide to other sectors of the economy.

A Few Interesting Perspectives About the ICs to be Used for IoT

In March 2016, in the technology quarterly issue of the magazine *The Economist*, Dr. Greg Yeric, a chip designer with ARM Inc., had the following things to share about the Integrated circuits (ICs) that would be used to usher in the upcoming IoT revolution. According to Dr. Yeric,

- The processors needed to make the IoT happen will need to be as cheap as possible.
- They will have to be highly energy efficient, and ideally able to dispense with batteries, harvesting energy from their surroundings, perhaps in the form of vibrations or ambient electromagnetic waves.
- They will need to be able to communicate, both with each other and with the Internet at large, using tiny amounts of power and in an extremely crowded radio spectrum.
- The chips that power the IoT will be built on much older, cheaper production lines.
- At the same time, though, the vast amount of data thrown off by the IoT will boost demand for the sort of cutting-edge chips.

These specifications highlight that IoT revolution would not only make use of analog sensors from older technology nodes but also drive a continuous growth in the economic demand for the latest and greatest transistor technology nodes driven by *More-than-Moore* and *Beyond CMOS*. In one way, the IoT revolution would involve a holistic approach toward the progress of Moore's law. In his own words, Dr Yeric says,

> If we really do get sensors everywhere, you could see a single engineering company—say *Rolls Royce* [a British manufacturer of turbines and jet engines]—having to deal with more data than the whole of *YouTube* does today.

In order to handle the Big Data traffic from so many sensors, the industry is also progressing to "Cloud." Cloud is the network of data centers that delivers services over the Internet. When computers were stand-alone devices, whether mainframes or desktop personal computers (PCs), their performance depended above all on the speed of their processor chips. Today computers have become more powerful without changes to their hardware. They can draw upon the vast (and flexible) number-crunching resources of the cloud when doing things like searching through e-mails or calculating the best route for a road trip. And interconnectedness adds to their capabilities: Smartphone features such as satellite positioning, motion sensors, and wireless-payment support now matter as much as the processor speed. For the IoT ecosystem, chips are now being designed specifically for cloud computing, neural-network processing, computer vision, and other tasks. Such specialized hardware will be embedded in the cloud, to be called upon when needed. Thus, the raw performance of end-user devices matters less than it did, because the heavy lifting is done elsewhere.

Designing a Holistic Ecosystem for the Fourth Industrial Revolution With *More-than-Moore* and *Beyond* CMOS

The advent of successful original equipment manufacturers (OEMs) like Apple Inc. has provided a rapid growth of System on Chip (SoC) devices. Such SoCs tend to devote around 65 percent of their real estate to memory, with the rest for everything else—including all the processor's logic gates, the necessary input/output circuitry, and numerous analog functions needed to run a phone, tablet, laptop, etc. While it is possible to shrink the size of the logic devices on SoC, the memory components do not scale anything like this and the analog circuitry barely scales at all. This means progress of Moore's law affects only a small portion of SoC. As such devices are never going to gain significant cost or performance benefits from shrinking further, and there is a good reason to stick with mature processes like 28nm (unless next technology node has proven to show a better yield), with their minimal cost when ushering in the IoT revolution. However, the IoT revolution has to ensure an overall growth of digital, analog, and mixed signal ICs leading to a broader technological and economic growth.

However, as explained in the preceding section, "Big Data" and "Cloud" would automatically drive the progress of *More-than-Moore* and *Beyond CMOS* drivers with an exponential growth in the volume of data from various sensors. In addition, according to the specifications put forth by Dr. Yeric, in order for the chips to be able to dispense with batteries and operate on tiny amounts of power, the IoT ecosystem should be able to interface with local "Cloud" as well as be able to transfer data over larger distances. Hence, while Internet would be able to connect the entire world and transform the data anywhere, the eco-system has

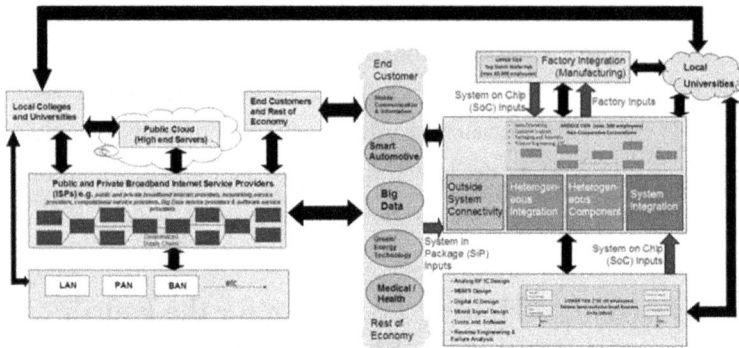

Figure 11.1 The entire semiconductor ecosystem for envisioning the Internet of things considering the new drivers for More Moore, More-than-Moore, and Beyond CMOS. (This figure has been repeated from Chapter 9 for convenience of the reader.)

to support a robust growth of local economy. In that regard, I propose a complete redesigning of the entire semiconductor ecosystem in order to adopt the ideas of *mass capitalism*, which will usher in an *economic democracy* with an *economic decentralization*. It would promote fair trade over free trade as well as focus on the economic growth by means of growing consumer purchasing power in the local economy.

When all of the above are taken into consideration and the newly designed ecosystem involves the drivers proposed by ITRS, the entire semiconductor and IoT ecosystem for ushering in the IoT revolution would look as shown in Figure 11.1.

Fundamental Factors of *Mass Capitalism* while Ushering in the Fourth Industrial Revolution of IoT

There exist five fundamental factors for success of *mass capitalism*. Let us elaborate these five fundamental factors as follows and verify whether the above-designed ecosystem complies with those five fundamental factors. Let us also understand the importance of having this type of ecosystem design in ushering in the fourth industrial revolution while implementing the drivers for *More-than-Moore* and *Beyond CMOS*.

1. For the semiconductor industry, the economic and monetary policy should ensure there is no valueless hoarding of wealth by a few

individuals, and this valueless hoarding should get converted into valuable investments for sustaining the progress of Moore's law to include *More-than-Moore* and *Beyond CMOS*.

2. There should be maximum utilization and rational distribution of all available resources, and nothing should remain unutilized for sustaining the progress of *More-than-Moore* and *Beyond CMOS*.

3. The business of operation for the semiconductor industry should be implemented in such a way that all potentialities of employees in semiconductor industry are properly utilized toward the success of their profession for driving *More-than-Moore* and *Beyond CMOS*.

4. The corporate human resources policies should be designed to encourage optimum utilization of all potentialities of employees for driving *More-than-Moore* and *Beyond CMOS*. However, there needs to be proper adjustments in utilizing these potentialities.

5. The process of utilizing employees' potentialities should not be the same for all employees of the semiconductor industry. Better methods of utilization should be continually developed, but the process of utilization should be progressive in nature. Time and space are changing, and the semiconductor industry will have to adjust with those changes. The principles of *mass capitalism* will not change; rather the application of these principles will have to adjust with the changing circumstances. The semiconductor industry will have to move forward by recognizing and adjusting with changes in time and space when driving progress of *More-than-Moore* and *Beyond CMOS*.

As shown in Figure 11.1, the proposed three-tier business model on the left-hand side for IoT and for the semiconductor industry on the right-hand side would ensure that there is a balanced economic growth. The supply and demand would rise and fall in proportion. Hence, during an economic downturn, there can be more R&D. The industry and academia conglomerates will prepare the future workforce for addressing the technological challenges. Although there can be both public as well as private "Cloud" services providers, in developing economies that lack sufficient capital, the local government has an important role to play in ushering in the IoT ecosystem. Besides, the presence of public Cloud servers will

ensure that continuous capital investments that are needed with the progress of *More-than-Moore* and *Beyond CMOS* are sustainable in the long run.

The public and private broadband ISPs (Internet services providers)
will offer competitive broadband Internet services and have decentralized
supply chains to ensure better collaboration between the service providers. The small businesses at the lower industrial tier will include local area
networks (LANs), broad area networks (BANs) as well as personal area
networks (PANs) which will offer two-way communication between the
end user and the rest of the IoT ecosystem through the middle industrial
tier. In this way, this three-tier business model for IoT ecosystem will
cater to the local customer and network him or her with rest of the semiconductor ecosystem.

The three-tier business model for semiconductor industry will incorporate all the specifications of the ITRS when it comes to *More-than-
Moore* and *Beyond CMOS*. The OEMs at the middle industrial tier would
have an exchange relationship in the form of a decentralized supply chain.
They would get the System in Package (SiP) inputs directly from the end
customer in order to offer customized electronic gadgets as per the needs
of the customers. These functionalities would include all the various drivers for *More-than-Moore* and *Beyond CMOS* as shown in Figure 11.1. The
OEMs will receive the inputs from the end customer and provide manufactured gadgets to them. In addition, the role of the middle industrial
tier for the semiconductor industry would be to interface with the IoT
ecosystem through the middle industrial tier and provide the necessary
supply of semiconductor ICs to the IoT ecosystem based on the requirements of the end users.

The lower industrial tier of the semiconductor industry will harness the
innovations of small businesses, which will include the design houses, contract third-party laboratories, test engineering facilities, etc. that offer innovative solutions to the middle industrial tier of the semiconductor industry.
As antitrust laws would be strictly enforced, it would prevent the formation of any industrial monopolies and preserve competitive capitalism at
lower industrial tier. The middle industrial tier will usher in collaboration
between the different businesses and the entire semiconductor ecosystem.
The SoC inputs to the semiconductor foundry will be provided by the
middle industrial tier based on the inputs received from the end customer.

The local engineering colleges and universities would provide a hands-on experience to create a workforce ready for the rapidly advancing semiconductor industry. The industry and academia conglomerates would also train the existing workforce to keep pace with the rapid technological progress in the semiconductor industry. As the semiconductor foundry would receive a financial backing from the local government, the operation of the semiconductor foundry would be sustainable. A compliance of the entire Industry 4.0 ecosystem with five fundamental factors of *mass capitalism* would ensure a minimum government intervention into the economy and offer a rational distribution of profits. The local colleges and universities would offer courses in analog design, mixed signal design, digital design, semiconductor processing, device physics, advanced package manufacturing, econometrics, data analytics, etc. These courses would be industry oriented and the faculty would be selected such that there are adjunct faculty members in the universities who have ties with the local IoT based companies and local semiconductor companies. This would help offer internship opportunities to graduate level students as well as offer a challenging thesis to PhD students that would not only offer them a doctoral degree but also help solve the problems of semiconductor industry in a cost-effective manner.

The engineering and management schools would inculcate the importance of collaboration in their courses and make it a prerequisite to have such courses for graduating students. This would usher in collaborative business models and collaborative corporate structures, collaborative R&D ventures, collaborative utilization of infrastructure and resources, collaboration between companies, academia, and government as well as collaboration between consumers and producers. In this way, the business model of industry would take into consideration the changes in the semiconductor industry and develop better methods of improving productivity and efficiency of workforce. *Mass capitalism* would ensure a rational distribution of wealth and lead to a broader economic growth by enabling a much larger number of people to participate in the resulting prosperity.

As the technology matures and new technology replaces the old, the proposed business model will prepare the overall industry for the changes happening at the macroeconomic level. In this way, the semiconductor industry would be able to adjust with the changes in time and space. It would help usher in the fourth industrial revolution of IoT by learning from the mistakes made with the third industrial revolution, which has resulted in an economic stagnation. As the designed holistic Industry 4.0 ecosystem will inculcate all the proposed drivers for *More-than-Moore* and *Beyond CMOS*, any new industrial revolution after the upcoming fourth industrial revolution would also become successful. In this way a New Golden Age would begin on Earth, bringing long-term prosperity to the human society. Although both the business models for the semiconductor industry on the right and for the IoT on the left are neo-fabless, by achieving collaboration across all sectors in the economy it would also become a virtual IDM business model for ushering in the fourth industrial revolution in the global economy.

Central Bank Monetary Policies under *Mass Capitalism*

The origins of negative interest rate of central banks like European Central Bank, Japanese Central Bank, etc. lie in the neutral rate identified by *Knut Wicksell* almost a century ago. Negative interest rates meant that the rate of interest required to bring an economy back to full employment with a stable inflation could be even negative. The real job creators in any free market economy are not only producers but also consumers. Hence, both producers and consumers have to prosper for a robust economic growth.

On macroeconomic level, there is a huge income inequality in global economy because of the reluctance of the central banks to follow a monetary policy that would usher in a true free market economy. The U.S. Federal Reserve (Fed) has also printed several trillion dollars in its ambitious Quantitative Easing (QE) program after the 2008 stock market crash that resulted in a global financial crisis. As a result, the economy stabilized in 2009 and began to grow in 2010.

However, the real wages of Americans fell, while the corporate profits skyrocketed. How did that happen? Because the entire increase in government spending from rising budget deficit went into the coffers of already wealthy producers. This is how *Goldman Sachs* alone could give bonuses of over $20 billion to its executives in 2009, while millions of ordinary Americans were still being laid off from their jobs. While the consumer debt actually fell, government spending and hence its debt actually rose so much that executives received hefty extra compensation.

Due to the absence of a free market economy where wages keep pace with productivity, the central banks have to print fiat currencies just to sustain deficits in respective economies. The trade deficits of the United States are a result of offshoring manufacturing jobs to Low Labor Cost (LLCs) Asian countries to increase the corporate profits of U.S.-based MNCs. With a lost domestic manufacturing in developed economies to countries in Asia, the citizens in developed countries are relegated to low-paying service sector jobs. Hence, the real wages of majority of citizens in the United States have actually decreased with rising trade deficits. These trade deficits, however, have benefited the external shareholders of corporations who have reaped huge profits from the rising share prices resulting from a practice of offshoring.

The growing economic disparity has also reduced the ability of low-wage-earning citizens to pay their fair share of income taxes. In addition, the tax cuts that are offered to corporations have added further to national budget deficits. Now, the growing trade and budget deficits can be sustained only by means of printing more currency. With their monetary policies, central banks like Fed or European Central Bank (ECB) print more money to bring down the rate of interest, and lower interest rates induce people to increase their borrowing or it increases consumer debt. As the wages fall with rising productivity, resulting from technological progress, the wage–productivity gap keeps rising so fast that even the government has to raise its own spending and debt constantly to sustain an economic demand from the growing gap between wages and productivity. In this way, even the national debt keeps rising because of increased government spending.

Hence, central banks keep printing more and more money and all the printed money keeps entering into the pockets of already wealthy individuals and corporations but such policies do not help boost domestic consumer purchasing power in economy. Hence, the real economic demand keeps stagnating and even falling in some cases. Since, wages contribute to economic demand and productivity contributes to an economic supply, wage–productivity gap contributes to demand–supply gap.

The Fed's benchmark interest rates are already close to 0 percent and just to keep the value of the dollar high in order to be able to export more goods to the United States, the ECB entered into a negative interest territory in June 2014. This unprecedented step of imposing a negative interest rate on banks for their deposits is in effect charging lenders to park money with the banks. In addition, the monetary policies of central banks let wages trail productivity resulting in a lack of economic demand. This causes all the money that is not put into the bank accounts to not get invested into the economy due to a poor economic demand. In fact, negative interest rates are causing money to get stashed underneath mattresses, thereby steadily shrinking the consumer credit in the economy.

When Fed hiked its benchmark interest rate by only 0.25 percent in early 2016, there was a net inflow of funds from developing economies into the United States. This move has strengthened U.S. dollar as compared to its other trading partners. The Asian trading partners like Japan are also following an unconventional monetary policy and Japanese central bank is moving into a negative interest rate territory just to maintain a net trade surplus with the United States. Hence, any reluctance by the Fed to hike its benchmark interest rate is undone by a decision of U.S. trading partners entering into a negative interest rate territory.

A rising value of U.S. dollar from all these policies is not good for the U.S. economy as the United States is unable to export its goods to other countries due to high value of U.S. dollar. Hence, U.S. trade deficits are steadily rising and could rise further if the Fed hikes its interest rates further in 2016. Rising value of the U.S. dollar combined with falling U.S. exports are crashing the profits of U.S.-based MNCs. All of this causes an inability of the United States to balance its budget in order to retain its AAA rating. The corporate bonds can no longer retain an excellent credit rating when corporate profits keep crashing because of falling consumer demand in the economy.

A net inflow of capital from developing economies into the United States has also triggered a panic in the developing economies as they are dependent on the capital arriving from developed economies for economic growth. The U.S.-based MNCs have neglected consumer demand in the U.S. economy, in search of a better return on investment (RoI) from Asian economies, and this is crashing multinational corporations (MNCs) profits in developing as well as developed economies. Everything depends on the ability of the United States to service its sovereign debt, which would no longer retain its AAA rating as corporate profits start crashing. The end result of all this would be exactly like what happened with the housing market crash of 2008, but this time the crisis will be much more severe than the housing market meltdown. Once the United States defaults on its debt, the global economy would collapse like a "Fire Cracker." The solution to this crisis is to reform monetary policies of central banks so that wages keep pace with productivity.

In his new book, *End Unemployment Now: How to Eliminate Joblessness, Debt and Poverty Despite Congress*, one of America's top economists, Professor Ravi Batra, argues that the trade deficit actually results from two forces: while the United States follows free trade, China and Japan do not. These nations constantly intervene in the market for foreign exchange and manipulate their exchange rates in order to cheapen their currencies relative to the dollar. A cheap currency means cheaper prices for its goods abroad. In his recent volume *End Unemployment Now, Batra* cites *Mass Capitalism* as *A Wave of the Future*, where I present solutions to the systemic problems caused at the macroeconomic level for the U.S. semiconductor industry as a result of America's free trade policies.

As explained by Professor Batra in this simple equation,

U.S. imports from China = China's imports from the United States + China's purchase of U.S. government bonds

If U.S. imports from China are $100 and China's imports from the United States are $30 but China spends $70 to buy U.S. government bonds, then of course China's ownership of U.S. debt will increase. The growing ownership of U.S. debt by China has caused a lot of geopolitical tensions. The growing wage–productivity gap in the United States, caused by its free trade policies—has resulted in a waning manufacturing sector in the U.S. economy. China also has a high wage–productivity gap, but they have avoided any overproduction of goods by having an exchange rate with the United States that creates an artificial demand for dollars. This way China has not followed true free trade and hence has prevented a depreciation of dollar in spite of rising U.S. trade deficits, but in this process China has become an increasingly larger withholder of U.S. national debt.

For the United States to eliminate its trade deficits and for manufacturing to make a comeback, it needs to follow the footsteps of China. It needs to manage its foreign exchange rate with the help of the Fed so that the Fed offers an incentive to Chinese importers to buy more American goods. *Professor Batra* explains in his latest book that this can be made possible by offering a better exchange rate like 4 Yuan for U.S. $1 or perhaps even 3 Yuan for U.S. $1. Let us take an example of an iPhone 6 manufactured in the United States. Let us suppose that the cost of an iPhone 6 is approximately $500. With the current exchange rate of 6 Yuan for U.S. $1, the cost of iPhone 6 to Chinese importer will be 3000 Yuan. Now, suppose the Fed offers an exchange rate for China as 4 Yuan for U.S. $1 instead of 6 Yuan for U.S. $1, then the cost of iPhone 6 to a Chinese importer would fall to 2000 Yuan from 3000 Yuan, which is a staggering 33 percent drop in price for the importer. If this does not work, the Fed can offer an exchange rate of 3 Yuan for U.S. $1 to increase U.S. exports to China.

The Chinese importers would also be delighted and there would be a rush to take advantage of Fed's offer. China will buy more consumer electronics from the United States. The United States will no longer run trade deficits but gradually also increase its exports to China. Eventually, American exports to China would soar to match its imports from China. This is how more manufacturing jobs can be created within the United States and trade deficits can be eliminated with existing free trade policies. The free trade policies do not let trade barriers to be imposed but allow exchange rate manipulation. *Professor Batra* argues that when China and Japan have pursued such policies, why can't the United States pursue similar policies to reduce its domestic poverty, debt, and joblessness?

These trade policies would rekindle America's waning semiconductor manufacturing base and create millions of high-paying semiconductor manufacturing jobs within the United States. The trade deficits would be eliminated without any major geopolitical tensions. There would be no import duty placed on Chinese and Japanese electronics entering the United States. However, with the growing consumer purchasing power in the United States, the quality of Chinese goods entering the United States would have to automatically increase. The problem of counterfeit electronics would be eliminated when domestic consumers would have sufficient buying power to demand good-quality electronics rather than cheap electronics. China's government should not resist this policy either, because Chinese exports to the United States would not be hurt, as a U.S. importer would still buy 6 Yuan for U.S. $1 from the People's Bank of China, and obtain Chinese goods at the same cost as before.

As long as all countries play by the rules, the process of offshoring manufacturing jobs just because of low costs in the third-world countries will also come to an end. These policies could be adopted by developing countries like India, which run a trade deficit with China and hence have a huge problem of domestic unemployment. Besides, China has also decided to compete with India's "Make in India" initiative to ensure that China retains its dominance as a global manufacturing hub. The Fed action would then create a free market outcome, even though in reality there still would be no actual free trade, which would make it mandatory for countries like China and Japan to abstain from intervention in markets. Once a balanced trade has been created between nations of the world, the economies can transition to *mass capitalism*-based free market economic reforms to further boost domestic purchasing power and hence increase domestic prosperity.

Conclusion

The upcoming fourth industrial revolution is very promising but it can become successful only after learning from the mistakes of the third industrial revolution and by means of establishing a holistic ecosystem that ensures long-term sustainability and profitability. The proposed business model also takes into consideration the contributions from *More-than-Moore* and *Beyond CMOS* in driving the economic growth and envisions these drivers as per the specifications provided by the ITRS. Such a neo-fabless three-tier business model or a virtual IDM business model would take the global semiconductor industry to its next level of innovation and financial success as it ushers in the fourth industrial revolution in the form of IoT.

Suggested Readings

[1] Mulay, Apek, *Mass Capitalism: A Blueprint for Economic Revival*, Book Publishers Network, Bothell, WA, 2014.
[2] Mulay, Apek, *Sustaining Moore's Law: Uncertainty Leading to a Certainty of IoT Revolution*, Morgan & Claypool Publishers, San Rafael, CA, 2015.

[3] The Economist, "*After Moore's Law: Double, Double, Toil and Trouble*", The Economist. March 12, 2016.

[4] The Economist, "*After Moore's Law: The Future of Computing. The Era of Predictable Improvement in Computer Hardware Is Ending. What Comes Next?*", The Economist. March 12, 2016.

[5] Mulay, Apek, "*Ballooning Deficit: Central Banks' Low Interest Rates Increase Liquidity but They Do Not Boost Growth*", DNA. April 29, 2016. http://www.dnaindia.com/analysis/column-ballooning-deficit-2207137

Dollars and Sense

Debating With the Internet of Things Experts

Introduction

I read an interesting article titled *The Internet of Things: 11 Experts on Business Opportunities*, which compiled opinions of 11 IoT experts about leveraging the various business opportunities in the Internet of things space. I would like to have a virtual sit-down with these experts and view their ideas from a macroeconomic perspective.

Virtual Sit-down With *Tony Fadell*, Founder of *Nest*

In a guest blog for the *Wall Street Journal* on the future of Internet, *Fadell* said,

> It took the telephone more than 45 years to earn a place in the majority of American homes. The Internet did it almost three times as fast. And yet, 4.4 billion people worldwide are still offline. Instead of seeking it out, we'll be surrounded by Internet in future. And instead of extracting data from it, we'll be fed a constant stream of curated, personalized information to help us solve problems and live better together.

While there is no doubt that the progress of Internet has been much faster than telephone, this has a lot of do with the lack of any kind of industry monopolies in the Internet domain. In case of standard voice telephony structure, the monopolies in telecommunications industry lobbied the U.S. government and United Nations International Telecommunications Union (ITU) to keep international calling rates high.

The only free market approach to get more people online is to create an ecosystem where the buying power of people grows in proportion to their productivity. While IoT would be able to feed abundant data to the end consumer, it wouldn't make any business sense if that information is provided for free. To make the business of Big Data sustainable, not only should there be an incentive for the providers to charge the consumer by means of providing more and more data but at the same time, consumers should also have a good buying power to be able to afford paying for the personalized information. This needs a true free market economy as well.

Virtual Sit-down With *Vala Afshar*, Chief Marketing Officer, *Extreme Networks*

In a blog for the *Huffington Post*, *Afshar* writes,

> All existing businesses must rethink their business models. Business models are shifting from discrete product sales, to recurring revenue models. Individual products no longer exist in a vacuum; interactions among devices from multiple sources and vendors must be understood and taken into account.

In order to keep the recurring revenue model sustainable, two things have to happen. First, consumer purchasing power in the economy should constantly grow so that these buyers can keep paying toward recurring revenue business models. Additionally, there have to be wide-ranging reforms in the financial industry, which encourage circulation of money and discourage accumulation of money. In this way, not only would purchasing power of majority in economy grow but, at the same time, there would be a multiplying effect resulting in appreciation of the value of currency. For a healthy interaction between devices from multiple sources, it needs a deep collaboration between businesses with symbiotic benefits.

Virtual Sit-down With *Guy Kawasaki*, Silicon Valley-Based Author, Speaker, and Entrepreneur

In an interview with the *Inc. Magazine, Kawasaki* said,

> "I want precise location outside of Bluetooth range. In a nutshell, I want Life360 for anything I stick a tracker on. It's not a matter of if, but when."

Kawasaki's ideas about being able to locate outside of Bluetooth range can only succeed if the supply chains that would usher in the IoT revolution can ensure that there is less to lose and more to gain by acting in the best interest of the supply chains. I have discussed it in the chapter titled "Design of Supply Chains for the Success of Internet of Things (IoT)"of my volume *Sustaining Moore's Law: Uncertainty Leading to a Certainty of IoT Revolution* (2015).

Virtual Sit-down With *Chris O'Connor*, General Manager, Internet of Things, IBM

In an *IBM* blog, *O'Connor* explained,

> Any company wanting to transform using IoT data needs to fully embrace the cloud. And because most enterprises have already fully embraced the cloud, the next step, and the new killer application for the cloud, is the Internet of Things. The only way to ensure that the IoT is an enabler rather than an obstacle is to engineer new products, operate existing products and gather data from connected interaction with a holistic IoT strategy in mind.

In my three volumes, I propose a wide-ranging macroeconomic approach to industrial policy (in this particular case, focused on the semiconductor portion of high tech, which is the foundation of all high-tech advancements and innovations) along with ideas to make it feasible to implement the next big thing of *IoT* revolution. Keeping a holistic IoT strategy in mind, my approach has been holistic in addressing economic, social, political, legal, and international trade issues in designing a robust ecosystem for IoT to flourish. Additionally, I have elaborated further on the IoT ecosystem in few chapters of this volume as well, thereby providing a blueprint for Industry 4.0 with *More-than-Moore* and *Beyond CMOS* drivers for the semiconductor industry.

Virtual Sit-down With *David Pogue*, Founder of *Yahoo Tech*

In an article for *Biz Journals*, Pogue said,

> UberX and AirBnB take it a step further by connecting you to everyday people for rides in the family car and overnight stays in a spare bedroom. I will never use a taxi again in one of the Uber cities.

> The recent cases of rape and sexual harassment of women in India who have used Uber's taxi services highlights the damage to the brand of any business when IoT-based software apps like UberX, etc. which are developed by one country are used in another country. This is similar to how globalization of semiconductor manufacturing has resulted in a national security threat for United States due to introduction of counterfeits into the U.S. supply chain. For IoT to truly prosper, IoT apps need to take into consideration the local economy, customs, and traditions and need to be able to comply with and enforce laws at local level. This is how IoT revolution could lead to local economic development around the world and would be able to connect nearly 50 billion devices worldwide in a sustainable way by year 2020.

Virtual Sit-down With *William Pence*, Executive Vice President and Chief Technology Officer, AOL

In an interview with *Medium*, Pence said,

> To say 'Internet of Things' is obligatory, but in the context of advertising it's very important. Look at the convergence of mobile

and commerce—NFC and mobile commerce and embedded sensors and beacons—notifications and promotions and highly personalized commerce will be a big part of that. The time is not far off where with a mobile phone you will get deeply contextualized promotions.

A highly personalized commerce along with mobile notifications and promotions is only possible with an ecosystem where the businesses make their decisions based on local information in order to cater to local economic needs. This calls for a wholesome decentralization of an economy while designing the IoT supply chains so that local businesses are most aware of local economic needs and cater to these needs offering not only notifications and promotions but even a very personalized commerce.

Virtual Sit-down With *Tom Black,* Vice President of IT and Enterprise Information Management, *Eaton*

Johnson Cornell University alumni and industry experts discussed Internet of Things. In this forum, *Black* placed his bet that startup companies will change the face of IoT. He said,

> Users are using the Internet to manage their lives. The complexities have come in because there are so many silos of data from a consumer point of view. No one is going to want to have 15 apps to control 15 appliances. I can guarantee that there will be startup companies that bring that together.

I would second *Black* in his view that startups have a big role to play in success of IoT revolution. The innovations come from startups and these innovations need to materialize for benefitting the economy at large. To create a robust growth of small businesses, major macroeconomic reforms have to be undertaken.

The growth of small businesses also depends on purchasing power in local economy. The higher the purchasing power of people in local economy, the more is their confidence in investing in the economy which in turn leads to economic growth. These investments would create greater demand for goods and result in creation of new businesses that would cater to those needs.

Additionally, startups developing apps to control a range of IoT appliances can be effective only with a deeper collaboration in the IoT ecosystem and ability of each app to symbiotically partner with a single app developer. No small business would let its IP be reused for free.

Virtual Sit-down With *Robert Scoble,* American Blogger, Technology Evangelist and Author

In an interview with *Forbes, Scoble* predicted what we can expect next with the wearable technology. He said,

> We are close to a second wave where we are going to have sensors that more accurately watch your activity while watching what is going on in the web stream. That is really where developers are going to get lit up. There is a shirt company that is making sensors that go into your clothing. They will watch how you sit, run or ski and give data on that information. There are even sensors coming that will watch your blood glucose level.

This forecast points to the exploding business prospect of data management as well as data analytics. While an application developer can get a breadth of useful information and can process that information in order to design several useful apps for the consumer, if the consumer does not have sufficient buying power, would he or she be able to afford to buy that personalized application?

No, unless global economy wishes to continue on the present unsustainable path of creating a debt-based economy, which has led us to present global macroeconomic crises. Hence, the IoT ecosystem should focus not only on the supply side of the economics but also on the demand side of the same to ensure that the resulting IoT revolution leads to a sustainable ecosystem.

Virtual Sit-down With *Brian Kelly*, Chief Technology Officer, *Golgi*

Brian Kelly discussed IoT over a homemade video mentioned in an article by *Arkenea*. *Kelly* suggests a potential fix for loophole in IoT technology as follows:

> When you are using the mobile device you are talking to a server that is accessible from anywhere but if you want to interact with a device that is in your home or enterprise that can be difficult to connect to, that's not a secured location that you can just make an inbound connection just there. Those kinds of scenarios are not encountered by mobile app developers. In order to solve this you need something in the middle that both mobile and that device can connect to.

While *Kelly's* ideas are thought provoking, they could be materialized in a three-tier business model presented in this volume, which is aimed at building robust growth of IoT sector. The other advantages of this model would be that it would lead to a balanced economic growth and result in a steady growth in consumer purchasing power in economy. The biggest macroeconomic advantage of the proposed new business model is that it would comply with the macroeconomic cycles of nature and thereby avoid creation of a huge unemployment during economic downturns.

Virtual Sit-down With *Jason Silva,* Filmmaker and Creator of Shots of Awe

In an interview given to the *Inc. Magazine*, *Silva* shares what captures his imagination in the Internet of Things space:

> Technology surrounding us with useful information, like a kind of "engineered serendipity." I'd like my smartphone to hear me when I say I'm hungry and recommend me a restaurant. I'd like to be serendipitously informed when a friend is nearby.

Silva's thoughts reinvigorate the importance of preserving Net neutrality for the success of IoT revolution. When the smart phone recommends a particular restaurant, even a small business should have a fair chance to make it to *Silva's* list of recommended restaurants. That would ensure a true free market competitive capitalism and elimination of all sorts of industry monopolies for success of IoT revolution.

Virtual Sit-down with *Laurel Papworth,* Social Media Educator

Papworth shared her views in Pew Research Center's report about IoT. She expressed how IoT will bring the next revolution in digital technology:

> Every part of our life will be quantifiable, and eternal, and we will answer to the community for our decisions. For example, skipping the gym will have your gym shoes auto tweet (equivalent) to the peer-to-peer health insurance network that will decide to degrade your premiums.

Laurel points to a very important role that would be played by IoT in ensuring fairness of the system. However, in order to make it practical, the global economy needs to transform from present individualized capitalism to a more collaborative capitalism where majority are the stakeholders toward the success of the ecosystem rather than a few minority. The ideas presented in my three volumes authored in three consecutive years 2014, 2015, and 2016 would help design such an ecosystem and eventually materialize *Laurel's* vision.

Suggested Readings

[1] Mulay, Apek, *Mass Capitalism: A Blueprint for Economic Revival*, Book Publishers Network, Bothell, WA, 2014.
[2] Mulay, Apek, *Sustaining Moore's Law: Uncertainty Leading to a Certainty of IoT Revolution*, Morgan & Claypool Publishers, San Rafael, CA, 2015.

Index

OTHER TITLES FROM THE ECONOMICS COLLECTION

Philip Romero, The University of Oregon and
Jeffrey Edwards, North Carolina A&T State University, *Editors*

- *U.S. Politics and the American Macroeconomy* by Gerald T. Fox
- *Seeing the Future: How to Build Basic Forecasting Models* by Tam Bang Vu
- *The Economics of Civil and Common Law* by Zagros Madjd-Sadjadi
- *Innovative Pricing Strategies to Increase Profits, Second Edition* by Daniel Marburger
- *Business Liability and Economic Damages* by Scott Gilbert
- *How Strong is Your Firm's Competitive Advantage, Second Edition* by Daniel Marburger
- *Eastern European Economies: A Region in Transition* by Marcus Goncalves and Erika Cornelius Smith
- *Health Financing Without Deficits: Reform That Sidesteps Political Gridlock* by Philip Romero and Randy Miller
- *Central and Eastern European Economies: Perspectives and Challenges* by Marcus Goncalves and Erika Cornelius Smith
- *Regression for Economics, Second Edition* by Shahdad Naghshpour
- *A Primer on Nonparametric Analysis: Volume I* by Shahdad Naghshpour
- *A Primer on Nonparametric Analysis: Volume II* by Shahdad Naghshpour
- *The Modern Caribbean Economy, Volume I: Alternative Perspectives and Policy Implications* edited by Nikolaos Karagiannis and Debbie A. Mohammed
- *The Modern Caribbean Economy, Volume II: Economic Development and Public Policy Challenges* edited by Nikolaos Karagiannis and Debbie A. Mohammed

Announcing the Business Expert Press Digital Library

Concise e-books business students need for classroom and research

This book can also be purchased in an e-book collection by your library as

- *a one-time purchase,*
- *that is owned forever,*
- *allows for simultaneous readers,*
- *has no restrictions on printing, and*
- *can be downloaded as PDFs from within the library community.*

Our digital library collections are a great solution to beat the rising cost of textbooks. E-books can be loaded into their course management systems or onto students' e-book readers.
The **Business Expert Press** digital libraries are very affordable, with no obligation to buy in future years. For more information, please visit **www.businessexpertpress.com/librarians**.
To set up a trial in the United States, please email **sales@businessexpertpress.com**.

www.ingramcontent.com/pod-product-compliance
Lightning Source LLC
Chambersburg PA
CBHW050110210326
41519CB00015BA/3900